Marxism and Leninism, Not Marxism-Leninism

Recent Titles in
Contributions in Political Science

MARXISM AND LENINISM, NOT MARXISM-LENINISM

An Essay in the Sociology of Knowledge

JOHN H. KAUTSKY

Contributions in Political Science, Number 335
Bernard K. Johnpoll, Series Editor

GREENWOOD PRESS
Westport, Connecticut • London

Library of Congress Cataloging-in-Publication Data

Kautsky, John H.
    Marxism and Leninism, not Marxism-Leninism : an essay in the
sociology of knowledge / John H. Kautsky.
      p. cm.—(Contributions in political science, ISSN 0147–1066;
no. 335)
    Includes bibliographical references (p.) and index.
    ISBN 0–313–29044–X (alk. paper)
    1. Socialism—History. 2. Communism—History. I. Title.
II. Series.
HX73.K375   1994
335.42′3—dc20   93–25074

British Library Cataloguing in Publication Data is available.

Library of Congress Catalog Card Number: 93–25074
ISBN: 0–313–29044–X
ISSN: 0147–1066

First published in 1994

Greenwood Press, 88 Post Road West, Westport, CT 06881
An imprint of Greenwood Publishing Group, Inc.

Printed in the United States of America

The paper used in this book complies with the
Permanent Paper Standard issued by the National
Information Standards Organization (Z39.48–1984).

10 9 8 7 6 5 4 3 2 1

To the
Department of Political Science at
Washington University in St. Louis

It is not the consciousness of men that determines their existence, but, on the contrary, their social existence that determines their consciousness.

Karl Marx

Contents

Preface

In this essay, I develop the argument that Marxism and Leninism are two quite different ideologies and counterpose this view to the commonly accepted one of Leninism as simply one form that Marxism took in the course of its evolution. That latter conception has led to much misunderstanding of both Marxism and Leninism and has been responsible for great confusion in the realms of both politics and scholarship.

My effort to bring clarity into this area rests on my conception of ideology. For the purpose of analyzing politics, that is, conflict among groupings of people with different interests and values, it seems to me appropriate to define an ideology with reference to the interests and values it expresses. I develop my conception of ideology, and of the role of words in it, as well as the defining characteristics of Marxism and Leninism that follow from it in chapter 1.

In chapters 2 and 3, employing a sociology-of-knowledge approach, I try to explain the appeal and the different meanings of the Marxian vocabulary, as it was used by Marxists and by Leninists, with reference to the position of labor in turn-of-the-century industrial Europe and of modernizing intellectuals in underdeveloped countries, beginning with turn-of-the-century Russia. As Marx was explicitly concerned with problems of industrialism rather than with those of underdevelopment, it is far less difficult to understand the appeal of his vocabulary in industrialized countries, like Germany and Austria, than in underdeveloped countries, like Russia and China. I shall therefore have to devote much less space to my analysis of Marxism than to that of Leninism and its non-Marxian policies clothed in Marxian words.

In chapter 4, I point out that in industrialized countries, notably in

Germany, France, and Italy, would-be Leninists could not be Leninists, which was true also in the Soviet Union in recent decades. In chapter 5, I seek to account for the origin and the persistence of what I regard as the misconception of Marxism and Leninism as a single ideology.

One reason for that misconception may be that scholars have usually discussed Leninism with reference either to European countries, including Russia, or to underdeveloped countries, but not to both. The former group does not see Russia as an underdeveloped country, and the latter does not link Marxism to Western labor movements. I have been fortunate that my research and teaching during the past four decades have been concerned with the politics of both industrialized and underdeveloped countries.

In particular, on the one hand, I have, from my intellectual beginnings, had an interest in Marxism and Western labor movements, some of it concentrated on the work of Karl Kautsky, as in my doctoral dissertation and more recently in my abridged edition of his magnum opus *The Materialist Conception of History* and my book *Karl Kautsky: Marxism, Revolution, and Democracy*. I thus developed a perspective on Marxism as quite distinct from Leninism, as it evolved from the theories of Marx and Engels into the thought and practice of social democracy, especially in Germany and Austria. On the other hand, I have in several books and some articles sought to analyze the revolutionary politics of underdeveloped countries, both in general and with special reference to Communism. I thus came to see Leninism and the Russian Revolution in that context and as quite distinct from Marxism.

While my argument in the present book is at most foreshadowed in one or two of my earlier writings, some of what I say here does, then, rest on research done in the past. I hope this will explain the all too numerous footnote references to my own writings. Embarrassed as I am by them, I thought they were preferable to summaries or restatements of what I had said and of data and literature I had referred to elsewhere. These would have been inappropriate in what was meant to be only a brief essay.

Finally, as this book was written and appears in the early 1990s, let me answer a question I have been asked a few times regarding my subject: Don't I know that Marxism and Leninism are now dead? Yes, I do know that, in important but different respects, both are substantially dead; and I even argue that both, for very different reasons, died long ago in most places where they had once been strong. I hope, however, that the entire essay negates the implication of the question that Marxism and Leninism are no longer worth analyzing and explaining. I respond to this implication specifically at the beginning of chapter 1.

Here, I offer two very general points in response. First, even if Marxism and Leninism were completely dead and even if they left no remnants or effects, which is obviously not true, it would be important to study them as major historical phenomena that powerfully affected the world at one time. Second, I deal here with ideas expressed in a single vocabulary but, analyzing their origins and appeals sociologically, can show that these ideas can best be seen as two quite different ideologies. My essay can thus serve as a case study in the sociology of knowledge, an approach that can be fruitfully employed in the analysis of all political ideologies. At the same time, the essay emphasizes and examines the function performed by words in Marxism and Leninism, a concern that should be equally relevant to the study of other ideologies.

I am grateful for their encouragement to Peter Schwartz and Serenella Sferza, who read an early draft of this essay, and to Sanjay Seth and Gary Steenson for their extensive critical comments on it, to which I tried to respond with some revisions and additions. Above all, I thank Jack Knight, Carol Mershon, and John Millett, and my son Peter Kautsky, for giving generously of their valuable time to help me with thoughtful understanding to improve my manuscript in many minor and some very major ways.

Having recently retired from, but continuing to work in, the Department of Political Science at Washington University in St. Louis, I dedicate this book to the Department, a remarkable institution consistently distinguished both by its academic and scholarly excellence and by its humane and pleasantly cheerful style. I owe an immense debt of gratitude to many of my past and present colleagues in it for offering to me, through more than half of my life, their warm friendship and colleagueship, their stimulation, collaboration, and support.

Chapter One

Introduction: Two Environments—Two Ideologies— One Terminology

Why Bother with Dead Marxism and Leninism?

The scholarly and journalistic literature commonly applies the single term "Marxism" to the thought and practice of such political thinkers and leaders as, among many others, Karl Marx and Friedrich Engels, Karl Kautsky and Rosa Luxemburg, Antonio Gramsci and Palmiro Togliatti, Maurice Thorez and Georges Marchais, V. I. Lenin and Leon Trotsky, Joseph Stalin and Nikita Khrushchev, Fidel Castro and Salvador Allende, Daniel Ortega and Abimael Guzmán, Mao Zedong and Deng Xiaoping, Ho Chi Minh and Pol Pot, Najibullah, Amílcar Cabral, and Mengistu Haile Mariam.[1]

Calling all these people Marxists, as they have called themselves, suggests that they share a common ideology and represent a single movement, a notion that appears to be widely, if vaguely, accepted. On the other hand, it seems obvious that huge differences divide some of these so-called Marxists, that particularly those near the beginning and those toward the end of the above listing have little, if anything, in common. Thus, it is difficult to conceive of Karl Kautsky in the context of Afghan politics or of an Ethiopian army colonel leading a mass labor movement like German social democracy.

By differentiating between Marxism and Leninism as distinct ideologies, this essay suggests a way of looking at this area of great intellectual confusion that may help to explain both the major differences among movements and regimes commonly referred to as Marxist and the fact that they can all think of themselves as Marxists and all speak, at least to some extent, the language of Marxism. I try to develop my explanation by taking a sociology-of-knowledge approach of relating ideology to its social environment, a perspective that seems generally in accord with Marx's view of ideology and may thus be particularly appropriate for a discussion of the Marxist and Leninist ideologies.

For my purposes here, I distinguish between two types of environments: industrialized and industrially underdeveloped. Ideologies that have proved to be widely appealing across many national and cultural boundaries must be explained with reference to broad types of societies. The dichotomy I draw between industrial and underdeveloped societies, though it obviously oversimplifies reality, is thus a useful one in accounting for the two ideologies I distinguish, each associated with one type of society. I also mention areas neither fully industrialized nor largely underdeveloped, like Italy of the 1920s or mid-twentieth-century Chile, with the composite ideologies of Gramsci or Allende that contain some elements of one ideology and some of the other.

I believe that my conception of two ideologies can serve to explain far more reality, and explain it better, and can bring more order into this area of the history of ideas and of political movements than can the notion of a single Marxist ideology from Marx to Mengistu or the possible alternative notion of dozens of different Marxisms.

But is this analysis still of interest when the death of Marxism and of Leninism is being proclaimed every day? As these lines are being written, the pictures and statues of Marx and Lenin are coming down in much of the world, Karl-Marx-Stadt is once again Chemnitz, and Leningrad is once again St. Petersburg. Is this essay then being rendered irrelevant by the dramatic events that have been taking place in the past few years in the Soviet Union and its successor states and in what used to be called its Eastern European satellites?

First, it must be noted that my argument that Marxism and Leninism are different ideologies implies that whatever the fate of one may be, the fate of the other is distinct from it. In my view, Marxism and Leninism changed for different reasons and in different ways, although both changed so drastically in important respects that one can fairly say that they have been dead for a long time.

What little Marxism there was in Russia died with Menshevism and the triumph of Leninism long ago. There having been no Marxism in the Soviet Union since then, recent events there prove nothing about the vitality of Marxism one way or the other. In the industrialized West, Marxism had directed its appeal to alienated industrial workers and promised to end their alienation. As their alienation was ended or at least reduced—though not only by the policies of Marxists—Marxism lost its appeal to workers and, in this sense, died.[2]

Similarly, Leninism committed suicide in Russia by the achievement of its goals. Leninism appeals to alienated intellectuals in underdeveloped countries and promises to bring them to power and to realize the rapid industrialization of their backward societies. When this was accomplished some decades ago in the Soviet Union and the other now industrialized countries of Eastern Europe, Leninism necessarily died.

What died only recently, then, as a result of the collapse of most Communist regimes, is not Marxism and Leninism but only their outward symbols: the pictures and statues, and also—except among a few hidebound leaders of surviving Communist parties—the vocabulary that Lenin had taken over from Marx.[3] That this Marxist vocabulary was used by both Marxists and Leninists is the principal reason for the assumption that Marxism and Leninism are one and the same ideology. To demonstrate that a single vocabulary can serve to express what are more usefully seen as two distinct ideologies is therefore a major objective of this essay.

Whether Marxism or Leninism is dead or alive, what I attempt here should be of some interest, for if my analysis is valid, it follows that a very widely held view that links or somehow identifies Western labor movements and their socialism with what also came to be known as socialism in the Soviet Union and Eastern Europe rests on a pervasive historical misunderstanding. This view not only has been accepted by scholars but came to play a prominent role in politics. On the one hand, it served the Right to attack the laborite and socialist Left in the West by identifying it with Communism in the East. On the other hand, it led some leftist advocates of pro-labor change in the West, for example, some French Communists and "marxisant" intellectuals, to associate themselves with or defend the Soviet regime. Indeed, the peculiar character of Communist parties in industrial Europe, as I interpret it in chapter 4, and possibly their very existence were in good part a result of this misunderstanding.

Communists and anti-Communists, some socialists, and many anti-socialists in the West as well as more or less neutral observers and, of course, the rulers of the Soviet Union, especially in its early years, have all helped perpetuate this misunderstanding. The misleading identification of Marxist "socialism" and Leninist "socialism" is likely to be with us for quite some time. A very few in the West will argue that labor should follow the Leninist path, because it was not Lenin, but Stalin and/or Mikhail Gorbachev, who failed in the Soviet Union, while very many others will say or imply that the failure of Communism in the Soviet Union discredits the programs and policies of Western Social-Democratic parties. In East Germany, where Social Democrats were strong before 1933, they have lost elections after the collapse of the Communist regime, no doubt in good part because voters resentful of that regime oppose the "Reds" and "socialism," symbols that Leninists and Marxists have shared.[4]

In any case, a reexamination of the relationship of Marxism and Leninism remains appropriate and even necessary because of their historical importance. There is a huge scholarly and popular literature that sees Lenin and his successors as the successors of Marx and Engels and regards Leninist or so-called socialist regimes in underdeveloped countries, beginning with the Soviet Union, as somehow resting on Marx's ideology and therefore as in some way related to the ideology of Marx's Social-Democratic successors. The conception of Marxism and Leninism as a single ideology has been so very widespread and influential among scholars and intellectuals, policymakers and the newspaper-reading public, and has caused so much misunderstanding of both Marxism and Leninism that an attempt to view it as a misconception and to explain how it arose and why it has remained so powerful would seem to be well worthwhile.

Two Ideologies

A political ideology, as I use the term here, is a view of the political world, involving description and explanation that may or may not be accurate from the perspective of an outside observer, as well as prescription, from a particular value position or point of view.[5] In the case of any one individual, that view may have been conditioned by all sorts of different factors involving the individual's experiences and personality. A widely held ideology, however, must express a widely held view conditioned by factors that affect great numbers of people in similar fashion. A political point of view is likely to be widely shared by people who occupy more or less the same position within a political and social system and share a common attitude toward that position or a common interest in preserving or changing it. That is the basic assumption underlying the argument in this essay.

In the next two chapters, I will link Marxism and Leninism to their respective social groupings in specific social environments. Here I must briefly define and distinguish between these two ideologies. One is the Marxism associated with the labor parties of the final decades of the nineteenth and the early decades of the twentieth century in industrial Europe, especially the German and Austrian Social-Democratic parties, that is sometimes referred to as the Marxism of the Second International. Marxism is one ideology in a broader category of laborite or social-democratic ideologies, all of which share a characteristic emphasis on the industrial labor movement and the improvement of the status of labor and on parliamentary democracy as a method and as a goal.

What distinguishes Marxism—though not necessarily very clearly— from other laborite ideologies, like British Fabianism, German Revisionism, or Scandinavian social democracy, is not only Marx's conception of history (of which his analysis of capitalism is a part) with its emphasis on class struggle and revolution, but also the specific vocabulary by which he expressed this conception. That vocabulary, however, employed to express a different conception, is used by Leninism as well. As my focus is on the distinction between Marxism and Leninism, and not between Marxism and other laborite ideologies, I cannot define Marxism with reference to the vocabulary it shares with Leninism, but I can define it with reference to its emphasis on labor and parliamentary democracy, which it shares with the broader category of laborite ideologies and which distinguish it from Leninism.

Leninist ideology is associated with revolutionary modernizing, antitraditional, and/or anticolonial movements in underdeveloped countries. It first appeared in turn-of-the-century Russia and also the Balkans, then in China, and has since inspired revolutionary movements in such nonindustrial countries as Vietnam and Cambodia, Southern Yemen and Afghanistan, Angola and Mozambique, Guinea-Bissau and Ethiopia, and, at least after the revolution, in Cuba. Its most outstanding thinker and founding father was clearly Lenin, and I therefore refer to this ideology as Leninism.

Leninism is one ideology in a broader category of modernizing ideologies, all of which share characteristic emphases on agrarian and anti-imperialist revolution, on the key role of intellectuals, and on rapid modernization. What distinguishes Leninism from other modernizing ideologies, like those represented by Jawaharlal Nehru or Gamal Abdel Nasser or, earlier, by the Mexican Revolution, is above all Lenin's use of Marx's vocabulary. Since it obviously does not distinguish Leninism from Marxism, and as I am not concerned with distinguishing Leninism from other modernizing ideologies, I define Leninism with reference to the characteristics it shares with the broader category of modernizing ideologies rather than with reference to its specific character (i.e., its vocabulary).

Leninism is, of course, all too generally referred to as Marxism, but I see these ideologies as belonging to two very different categories, and each of their founding fathers is associated with one of these. Just as the term Leninism is, in everyone's mind, linked to the thought of Lenin, so I am using the term Marxism, as it once was but is evidently no longer generally employed, to point to a linkage with Karl Marx's thought. That makes it impossible to refer to Stalin, Mao, or Mengistu as a Marxist, as is so often done, for the thought and the policies of such revolutionary leaders reflected not Marx's laborite thought but Lenin's modernizing one.

The following matrix may help clarify what different ideologies, including Marxism and Leninism, have in common and what distinguishes them.

	LABORITE IDEOLOGIES for advancement of industrial labor and parliamentary democracy in industrial countries	MODERNIZING IDEOLOGIES for intellectual-led anti-traditional and anti-colonial revolution and rapid modernization of underdeveloped countries	

MARXIST
 	
TERMI-
 	
NOLOGY
	Marxism
	
	Marx, Engels
	  Kautsky, Luxemburg
	  Bebel, Adler
	   Hilferding, Bauer
	    Togliatti
	     (Brandt, Kreisky)
		Leninism
		
		Lenin
		  Trotsky, Stalin
		   Mao, Ho, Pol Pot
		    Cabral, Mengistu
		     Najibullah
		      Castro, Guzmán	

NON- MARXIST TERMI- NOLOGY	Fabianism Bernstein Jaurès Scandinavian Social-Democracy	Sun Cárdenas Nehru Nasser	Kemal Paz Sukarno Nkrumah

As I seek to explain the thought of ideologists with reference to their sociohistorical setting rather than their personal character or intelligence, I am not arguing that the laborite Marxists were closer to Karl Marx's thought than Lenin and his followers because they were more upright and honest or more insightful and scholarly. Rather, the social-democratic and laborite Marxist ideologists were closer to Marx than ideologists in underdeveloped countries could be because the industrial environment to which they were responding was closer to the one to which Marx had responded, especially during the last three decades of his life. After all, ideology as a conceptual apparatus is wedded to the ideologist's experience, and ideology as a moral perspective is wedded to his or her task or mission.

Marx and Marxism

A few remarks are in order here to explain why I include Karl Marx's thought and Marxism among laborite and social-democratic ideologies.

To associate Marx with Marxism rather than with Leninism, as I have now defined these ideologies, I do not need to become involved in the endless and fruitless debates of the past hundred years as to what constitutes "true" Marxism. I merely need to point to the undeniable fact that most of Marx's work is focused on the development of industrial capitalism and of the industrial working class, and very little of it on problems of underdevelopment and colonialism, many of which did not arise until well after his death.[6] If I refer to Marxism as "laborite" as well as social-democratic, this is not to suggest that it was the ideology of narrow trade unionism, concerned only with workers' short-term interests, but simply to stress its link to labor as one of the major characteristics distinguishing this ideology from Leninism.

Marx's attitude toward parliamentary democracy, as distinguished from that of Marxist parties functioning after his death, is not as clear as his interest in the proletariat, for in his lifetime substantial legal labor parties hardly existed and most parliaments, including the House of Commons, were not yet elected by universal suffrage. The French and Swiss parliaments, elected by universal manhood suffrage, represented still overwhelmingly nonindustrial populations, and the imperial German Reichstag was largely powerless. Thus, the question of labor playing an effective role in parliaments did not arise for Marx, but he clearly did favor majority rule and universal suffrage.

Friedrich Engels, who had collaborated closely with Marx for four decades and survived him by twelve years, was intimately involved with the early Social-Democratic parties, especially the German party led by August Bebel and also the Austrian one led by Victor Adler, and approved of their participation in electoral and parliamentary politics.[7] Marxist Social-Democratic parties were henceforth, throughout their century-long history, strong advocates and defenders of parliamentary democracy with universal suffrage.

It can be argued that Marxist ideology should not be considered "laborite," because to Marx and his followers the ultimate goal was the "emancipation" of all of humanity, not merely of the working class. However, their concern with human liberation from all kinds of oppression and discrimination was hardly more than a vague ideal. It was quite secondary to their concern with industrial labor, for they saw human liberation as a necessary consequence of socialism—often simply because they defined socialism to encompass it—and they regarded the working class as the instrument that would bring about socialism. Already in the *Communist Manifesto*, Marx and Engels saw the proletariat as the only revolutionary class and asserted that its victory must bring the end of the oppression of women and of hostility between nations. While racial and ethnic discrimination and the position of women were given relatively little serious thought, the organization and education or indoctrination of labor and the improvement of its condition were of the greatest importance to Marx and to Marxist parties. In this sense they were, indeed, laborite.

Although I emphasize its laborite component here, it goes without saying that Marx's thought did not deal only with the working class and that he contributed to and influenced many intellectual currents. As a result, many thinkers—Lenin, of course, included—some of whom might have had no interest in industrial labor at all, could, if they so choose, trace their intellectual descent back to Marx. Here, however, I am not concerned with the many ideas Karl Marx contributed or stimulated or with the many intellectuals who, working in different fields, may have thought of themselves or have been thought of as Marxists. I am not concerned with "Marxism" in this sense.

The Marxism that is my subject here is the broad stream of thought that runs from Marx and Engels through the "classical" or "orthodox" Marxism of Karl Kautsky (who was close to Engels) and the Austro-Marxists, like Otto Bauer and Rudolf Hilferding (who were close to Kautsky), and through the history of the German and Austrian Social-Democratic Parties. Some of the elements of this stream have been gradually diluted, but what I regard as its defining characteristics have never disappeared. Western Social-Democratic parties continue to be linked to industrial labor movements and to champion their interests, and, of course, to participate in electoral and parliamentary politics. They no longer call themselves "Marxist," however, and much of Marx's vocabulary and analysis is no longer appropriate to their needs and has been abandoned.

Confusingly, the designation "Marxist," given up by social democrats, has been successfully claimed by Leninists and, more recently, also by thinkers often labeled "Western Marxists."[8] Marxism and social democracy, have, then, come to be regarded as distinct and even mutually exclusive or hostile ideologies. I shall nevertheless refer to the particular Western social-democratic laborite ideology that I need to distinguish from Leninism, as Marxism, because, across obvious differences reflecting major changes in the position of labor in industrial societies, there runs a straight line from Marx and Engels to Willy Brandt and Bruno Kreisky. On the other hand, there is no line from Marx to Mao and Mengistu; rather, a new line begins with Lenin and runs to more recent revolutionaries in underdeveloped countries. For now, I will simply assert this certainly highly controversial point. Much of the rest of this essay will, I hope, serve to support it.

One Terminology

That laborite Marxism and modernizing Leninism are very different is not news. Their differences emerged in the conflicts between Mensheviks and Bolsheviks and became particularly clear in the polemics of Kautsky and Lenin during and after World War I and the Russian Revolution. Much of the time since then, Social-Democratic parties and Communist parties professing to be Leninist have been bitter enemies. In the period since the 1950s, when Social-Democratic parties have no longer employed Marxist terminology, the differences have been even more obvious.

The point of this essay is not to show that Marxism and Leninism, as I have defined them, are different because they evolved in different directions from common beginnings. It is, rather, to argue that, from their respective beginnings in Marx and Engels and in Lenin, Marxism and Leninism have *always* been different ideologies, different views shaped not just by different interpretations of Marx's thought but also in response to different environments by people in different positions. With respect to the policies in fact pursued by the adherents of the two ideologies, the differences between them seem quite obvious, but they have been concealed from the adherents of both ideologies themselves, and from neutral as well as biased commentators down to the present, by the powerfully confusing fact that the two ideologies are couched in the same terminology.

This is, of course, due to the fact that Lenin, who formulated thoughts and pursued policies appropriate to a revolutionary modernizer in an underdeveloped country, had early in his political career come under the influence of Marx and Engels, of German Social Democrats, and of Russian Marxists influenced by these Western laborite thinkers. Thus Lenin and his followers came to use the vocabulary of Marx and to see their underdeveloped environment in terms of the concepts used by Marx and the German Social Democrats with reference to their industrial one.[9] Words and concepts like capitalism and socialism, bourgeoisie and proletariat, class struggle and revolution are central in both ideologies, at least in the earlier stages of their development.

Once Lenin and his revolution had triumphed, his terminology, like his Party, became established in a monopolistic position. Lenin's successors and the new generation they created by modernizing Russia were, as Lenin himself had been, unable to think in any language other than that of Marxism. All domestic and foreign policies pursued by the Soviet government during the next seven decades were described in Marxian terms, much as their substance necessarily differed from what Marx could have had in mind. Thus, the ruling Party was identified with the "proletariat," opposition to it was called "bourgeois," and fighting the opposition was seen as "class struggle"; turning an agrarian into an industrial society was thought of as "building socialism," and the establishment of bureaucratic control over industry and agriculture involved in this process was called "socialization" and "collectivization"; and the promised future society was always referred to as "socialism" and "communism."

If an ideology is defined with reference to the words and concepts it employs, then Marxism and Leninism are, indeed, a single ideology. For my purposes of political analysis, however, I define an ideology differently. If thinkers like Lenin and Kautsky could read the same words in the same writings of Marx and use them to justify and describe quite different policies, I see them here not as arriving at different and more or less "correct" interpretations of a single ideology of Marxism, but as thinkers in different positions with different political needs responding to different political situations in different environments—in short, as representatives of different ideologies.

That I do not define an ideology with reference to the words in which it is expressed by no means implies that these words are not important, that they make no difference in politics. As I will stress in a moment, they can be immensely important; but if the same words and concepts, appearing in different environments, represent and appeal to different kinds of people, if they serve different interests and functions, then, according to my definition of an ideology, the single vocabulary gives expression to different ideologies.[10]

Ideology and Words

Ideology plays a vital role in affecting and conditioning political behavior. No one acts politically—no one advocates a policy, becomes or supports a politician, joins an organization, votes, rebels—without some thought motivating his or her behavior, and that thought is ideological, it is a response to the outside world from a particular political point of view. If one sees politics, as I do, as conflict of interest, and if one interprets interests broadly to include relevant values, attitudes, and sympathies, then one cannot conceive of politics without ideology, for ideology is merely an expression of interests.

Ideology, then, in good part explains politics, but ideology is itself subject to explanation and can, in good part, be explained with reference to social structure. As a view held in common by many—though of course not all—people occupying similar positions in a given society, it is a necessary aspect of a given social structure.

Thus, the growing labor movements of the late nineteenth and early twentieth centuries in the most advanced industrialized countries of Europe, given the position they occupied in their political systems (as I will describe it in chapter 2), *had* to adhere to one ideology or another in the broader category of laborite ideologies. They had to be attracted by its advocacy and prediction of the advancement of industrial labor and of the achievement and use of parliamentary democracy.

Within the broader category of laborite ideologies Marx formulated a much more specific and coherent body of thought by linking it to ideas and insights in the social sciences, especially economics, and to a conception of history, all of which made Marxism particularly attractive to intellectuals. As his conception of history emphasized overt conflict, particularly class struggle and revolution, it proved to be appealing in the authoritarian empires of Central Europe, where the political position of the labor movements seemed to make such concepts relevant. Thus, as I will show in chapter 2, it was Marxism, the laborite ideology as expressed specifically in Karl Marx's thought—and in his terminology— that became influential especially in the German Empire. That it was influential there greatly affected the political behavior both of its ad- herents and of their opponents, but *that* Marxism was influential in the German Empire was a result of the social structure of that empire and, more specifically, of the respective positions in it of labor and of the government and its supporters.

Just as European labor movements had to adopt what I define as a laborite or social-democratic ideology at one stage of their development, so movements of intellectuals in underdeveloped countries *had* to adhere to a modernizing ideology, Leninism being one of these. They had to do so, given the position of intellectuals in their societies and given their interests developed in response to the impact of modernization coming to their countries from without, as I will analyze them in chapter 3. The revolutionary movements that accepted the Leninist ideology were a result not so much of this ideology as of the social structure of their countries and the place of intellectuals in it.

Not only ideologies but also their specific vocabulary can affect politics, for when people think, and thus motivate their political behavior, they shape their thoughts in the form of words. It was not just Marxism but the Marxian word "revolution" that played a role in the politics of the German Empire, mobilizing both support and opposition. The conflict between German Marxists and Revisionists at the turn of the century turned in part on the questions of whether their Party was "revolution- ary" and even, quite explicitly, whether it ought to use the word "rev- olution" in its propaganda.

The Marxian vocabulary Lenin employed to express his modernizing ideology also affected politics in some ways that a different vocabulary expressing similar modernizing ideologies did not. At least the fact that his thought with respect to industrialized countries was couched in Marxist concepts had major consequences. Lenin looked to such coun- tries in Central and Western Europe for support among their workers and for opposition on the part of their bourgeoisie, an expectation that proved to be partially self-fulfilling. That some workers and intellectuals in these countries now expressed their interests by thinking of them- selves as Leninists and that some more conservative groups expressed theirs by attacking Leninism was due to the fact that Lenin used the terminology of Marx. The interests these people expressed in this fashion were, however, shaped by their positions in their societies. It was these positions that made Lenin's Marxist language attractive or threatening to them.

Of course, there are limits to what words can do. All of Lenin's talk about the bourgeoisie and capitalism could not make turn-of-the-century Russia into a highly industrialized country, just as his constant references to the proletariat and socialism could not produce a highly organized mass labor movement that could take power and then restructure Russian society in labor's interests. Lenin and Leninist modernizing movements, regardless of their vocabulary, had to react to their underdeveloped environment much as non-Leninist modernizing movements did.

Still, politics is carried on largely through the use of words, and those engaged in politics respond to each other's words as well as to each other's policies and behavior, which are, indeed, difficult to distinguish from the words used to describe them. The responses to words may consist not only of more words but also of substantive behavior. The mere fact that Smith says to Jones that he will hit him, may cause Jones to hit Smith.

Words obviously have consequences, then. If the words are descriptively inaccurate and inappropriate, as is the Marxian vocabulary used by Leninism in conditions of underdevelopment, they can become myths, that is, false beliefs that inspire behavior on the part of those who accept them. Words thus can even function in self-fulfilling fashion. Lenin's words could not create a powerful proletariat, a proletarian revolution, or a proletarian regime in Russia, but they could turn some Western capitalists into his enemies and some Western workers into his supporters, thus fulfilling some of his predictions. And the behavior and the words of these capitalists and these workers, in turn, reinforced the myth of the proletarian character of Leninism. This is a matter I will discuss in chapter 4.

Chapter Two

The Evolution of Marxism

SOCIALIST LABOR MOVEMENTS

Origins

The rise of socialist labor movements in Western Europe in the nineteenth century can be explained as a reaction to the growth of capitalist industry. The latter development is, no doubt, a necessary condition for the rise of these movements, but, as the growth of capitalist industry without a concomitant socialist labor movement in North America suggests, it is not a sufficient one. While several factors help account for the absence of such a movement in North America, it would seem that it is only industrial capitalism developing in a sociopolitical environment hitherto dominated by an aristocracy that produces socialist labor movements as a response.

The growth of new industrial classes within an agrarian society with age-old rigid class divisions and distinct class cultures, where individual status was largely determined by class membership, could hardly occur without friction. It was a relatively smooth process for the new industrial bourgeoisie, initially because it grew gradually out of the established classes of merchants and artisans and later because its new wealth permitted it to buy its way into the upper strata of society. Businessmen could buy landed estates and affect an aristocratic life-style, they could send their children to the schools of aristocrats and marry into their families, they could even buy aristocratic titles. At the same time, though often only slowly and reluctantly, aristocrats went into business.

To some degree, then, more so in Britain than on the Continent and with much mutual resentment along the way, the old and the new upper classes came to merge socially. Everywhere in Europe they eventually merged politically, as the bourgeoisie tended to join the aristocracy in the face of rising labor opposition.

The new industrial workers were recruited largely from the peasantry, the class least prepared for change in the preindustrial order. Abruptly, sometimes literally overnight, transplanted into a new urban environment and an industrial way of life, they could not fit into any of the still accepted class categories of the old agrarian society. Cut off physically from their peasant roots, looked down upon by the property-owning petty bourgeoisie of craftsmen and shopkeepers, far removed from the bourgeoisie and the aristocracy, miserably poor, they were discriminated against, isolated, and excluded from established institutions.

Unlike American workers, who developed in a society without a feudal background, European workers were constantly confronted by the fact that they could not vote in elections or join certain organizations, that they could not attend certain schools or pursue certain careers *because* they were workers. They could thus hardly help becoming aware that they were, indeed, workers and, as such, different from other people. They could not help becoming class-conscious, just as a black person growing up in the United States cannot avoid becoming conscious of being black and of having something important in common with other African-Americans.

As a large and rapidly growing class of people, thrown together in crowded slums and factories and sharing certain common interests, workers could hardly remain isolated. They responded to their exclusion from the established institutions of society by forming their own institutions and, to some extent, their own culture. Their organizations included not only (as they did in the United States) trade unions to represent workers as employees in particular trades or industries vis-à-vis their employers but also women's and youth organizations, sports clubs, hiking clubs and choral societies, educational and cultural institutions, libraries, publishing houses and newspapers, consumer cooperatives and political parties with active local organizations. Many of these organizations were overlapping and interconnected. Many, like unions and parties, sponsored others and imbued them with a common ideology. All of them aimed at improving the lives of workers not only materially but also by giving them some sense of their importance, power, and dignity, which the larger society denied them.[11]

All such organizations may have presupposed a degree of class consciousness in order to be established, but, once established, they certainly reinforced class consciousness and, indeed, helped create it for subsequent generations of workers. In imperial Germany, it was said that workers were born into and died in the Social-Democratic movement, which, far more than a mere political party, encompassed all the many different types of workers' organizations. To many, it must have seemed that to be a worker and to be a Social Democrat was one and the same thing, that there was no alternative to being both.

The Appeal of Marxism

In this situation in Western Europe and particularly in Germany—the rest of the Continent was by and large slower to industrialize—the early labor movements, and especially intellectuals attached to them or in sympathy with them, could easily be attracted to Karl Marx's thought. Itself a reaction to early industrialization, its view of the proletariat as a sharply distinct class destined to play a central role in the history of the future could seem highly relevant to them. To a deprived, down-trodden minority, the promise of an inevitable victory over its enemies and a future of material abundance and a better life was bound to be appealing. This was all the more true as, in an age when science in general and Darwinist evolutionary thought in particular enjoyed great prestige, the promise rested on a supposedly scientific basis and not mere wishful thinking.

Moreover, the Marxian prediction of the growth of labor in terms of numbers, organizational strength, and class consciousness was strikingly confirmed by actual developments, which further strengthened its appeal. Now that, in recent decades, these Marxian predictions have no longer been valid, it is all too easy to underestimate not only the intellectual power required to formulate them in the mid-nineteenth century but also the immense confidence in the inevitability of a triumph of socialism that they could inspire.

Marx's prediction of the irresistible rise of labor to ultimate victory should have met the needs of and been appealing to the labor movement in Britain as well as on the Continent. Indeed, the prediction was based in part on Marx's study of British capitalism. But in his thought and in his terminology—which changed less in the course of his lifetime than his thought—the rise of labor was associated with growing conflict—class struggle—culminating in a violent or nonviolent revolution. These elements of Marxism were derived from Marx's early experience in Germany and his study of recent and current French history; he was, after all, born only twenty-nine years after the outbreak of the French Revolution and witnessed several revolutionary upheavals in France.

In Britain, Marx's emphasis on class struggle and especially on revolution seemed rather irrelevant and hence was not appealing. Here trade unions of skilled workers could for some time collaborate with and work within the business-dominated Liberal Party. When, after the rise of the New Unionism at the end of the nineteenth century, unions did, at the beginning of the twentieth, form the Labour Party to secure independent labor representation in the House of Commons, British workers, though highly class conscious, had little doubt that the road to power for them was open and led through elections and Parliament.

The situation was different on the Continent, though of course Marxism fared quite differently in different countries there. I attempt here to explain its appeal only in Germany, the country where it was most successful. Much of my explanation will also be relevant to Austria, parts of which became industrialized not much later than Germany and which went through similar political phases of an aristocratic-military monarchy until 1918, a first republic until 1934, a period of fascism—four years clerical and seven years Nazi—until 1945, and a second republic since then.

By the turn of the century, the German and Austrian Social Democrats had grown into mass labor parties, the only labor parties in their countries. They were united and had explicitly Marxist programs and leaders who considered themselves faithful Marxists. In then industrially more backward France and Italy, there was no mass labor movement comparable in size and strength to the German and Austrian ones. French and Italian socialists had to compete for labor leadership with nonsocialists, such as syndicalists, and were themselves plagued by splits and factionalism; and the socialist leaders and programs were not necessarily all faithful to Marxism.

The German and Austrian Social Democrats, then, were clearly labor parties and clearly Marxist, while the French and Italian labor movements were not all socialist and the socialists were not all linked to labor or all Marxists. Since my concern here is with Marxism and, in order to distinguish it from Leninism, particularly with Marxism's link to labor, the German and Austrian labor movements are more relevant than the French and Italian ones. I shall turn to France and Italy in chapter 4, where I discuss their Communist Parties to raise the question whether there could be Leninism in industrial Western Europe.

THE SOCIAL-DEMOCRATIC PARTY IN THE GERMAN EMPIRE

Growth and Weakness

In the German Empire, there was no strong liberal party like the British one, no strong commitment to democratization in the newly growing bourgeoisie. German unification had failed under bourgeois auspices in 1848 and had been accomplished under Prussian aristocratic ones in 1870–71. Big business interests represented in the National Liberal Party were mostly allied with the aristocratic Conservatives in support of the imperial government. That government rested immediately on the military and the bureaucracy but more broadly on the "marriage of iron and rye" of the "Ruhr barons" and the Prussian Junkers, based on common interests in a protective tariff, colonial and naval expansion, and strong opposition to the rapidly rising labor movement.

Thus, while in Britain labor could exploit the rivalry between Conservatives and Liberals and obtain concessions from both, as with respect to suffrage, in Germany labor found itself isolated not only socially, as it was in Britain, but also politically. Its response was the formation of an independent labor party. Two smaller parties, founded in the 1860s and led, respectively, by Ferdinand Lassalle and by Wilhelm Liebknecht and August Bebel, united in 1875 into what became the Social-Democratic Party (SPD), three decades before the formation of the Labour Party in industrially more advanced Britain.

The SPD was repressed (except in the Reichstag) under Bismarck's anti-Socialist law (1878–90), and it remained discriminated against and was treated as a semisubversive organization until the end of the Empire in 1918.[12] Its members could not be, and its voters were not supposed to be, civil servants, teachers, or professional soldiers and reserve officers, and restaurants where they met were "off limits" to soldiers for being "frequented by prostitutes, pimps and Social-Democrats."[13] This, even though it was the single largest party in terms of popular votes in the Empire beginning in 1890 and polled roughly one-third of all votes in national elections beginning in 1903.

William II referred to Social Democrats as "*vaterlandslose Gesellen*," and German chancellors and other politicians used similar language, reading them out of the fatherland and, incidentally, agreeing with the *Communist Manifesto* that "the workingmen have no country [*Vaterland*]." Though it turned out in 1914 that, contrary to William and Marx and Engels, German workers were quite patriotic, it is not surprising that Marx's doctrine of class struggle, of workers having interests sharply distinct from those of the ruling classes, seemed relevant in the German Empire and had wide appeal in its labor movement.

The SPD's remarkable growth (from about 125,000 votes, 3.2 percent of the total vote, in 1871, to 4,250,000, 34.8 percent of the total vote, in 1912) was made visible in the elections to the Reichstag by universal manhood suffrage. Its representation in the Reichstag, however, was severely limited both by the electoral system and by the failure to redistrict. The system of runoff elections tended to favor the anti-socialist parties and voters who could combine against the SPD on the second ballot. That electoral district lines were not redrawn in over four decades of rapid urbanization also put the disproportionately urban-based SPD at a severe disadvantage.[14] Thus, the proportion of seats the Social Democrats obtained in the Reichstag was usually about half or one-third of the proportion of the votes it won, while the Conservatives were significantly and increasingly overrepresented after all elections but two early ones; and they, as well as the National Liberals, needed, on average, about one-third as many votes to gain one seat in the Reichstag as the SPD.[15]

Even if the Social-Democratic Party had won popular majorities in elections to the Reichstag—something that, in fact, it never came close to achieving—and even if it had somehow won a majority of the seats in the Reichstag, it is not at all clear, as it was under the British parliamentary system, how it could have come to power—that is, how it could have gained control of the executive. The constitution did not provide for such control by the Reichstag, and in Prussia, which included nearly two-thirds of the population of the Empire, the blatantly discriminatory three-class suffrage was retained until 1918.[16] The monarchical regime was determined to keep what it regarded as the enemy of the state out of power. It was a powerful regime that could rely on a loyal and well-disciplined military and bureaucracy, and it enjoyed the support not only of the agrarian and industrial upper classes but also of broad strata in the middle classes and the peasantry. It derived its legitimacy both from monarchical and aristocratic traditionalism and from the fact that both the successful unification and the industrialization of Germany had taken place under its auspices.

The labor movement in the German Empire, then, faced an ambiguous situation. On the one hand, there was its steady, impressive growth; on the other hand, there was the powerful, indeed the seemingly insurmountable, opposition to the achievement of its goals. To this situation there corresponded two striking characteristics in the thought of Social Democrats, particularly of their leadership and among their intellectuals.

On the one hand, they were inspired by indomitable optimism; there was no doubt in their minds that they would come to power—not today or tomorrow, but in the not-too-distant future. They simply took it for granted—not unreasonably, in light of their experience—that advancing industrialization would produce more and more workers and that these would necessarily become Social Democrats. On the other hand, SPD leaders and thinkers could not visualize, let alone plan for, any way of coming to power. Neither the method of gradual advances through trade union pressure and hoped-for political reforms nor that of more or less violent confrontations with the regime, as through mass strikes—both of which had advocates in the SPD at various times—offered practical prospects of success. Paradoxically, Social Democrats had good reason both for their optimistic expectations and for their inability to put them into effect or even to know how to do so.

Revolution and Marxism

Under these circumstances the Marxian concept of revolution proved to be particularly appealing. Of course, not all German workers or even all socialist workers were isolated and alienated from the broader culture to the same degree,[17] nor was there any kind of unanimity among German Social Democrats, either in the rank and file or among the leaders and intellectuals, as to the SPD's policies and goals and its "revolutionary" character. I am about to stress socialists' emphasis on the latter, only because my object here is not to present a well-rounded picture of attitudes prevailing among workers or in the SPD, but to explain the appeal of Marxism to the German labor movement and to point out the functions that the key Marxian concept of revolution served for it.

In Marx's conception of history, the proletarian revolution and its ultimate victory are inevitable, a prediction that seemed confirmed by the growth of the labor movement and its organizations and, in turn, no doubt helped promote that growth. If this promise involved in the concept of revolution corresponded to and also inspired the SPD's optimism as to its inevitable ultimate victory, the concept was, on the other hand, sufficiently vague to correspond to and also conceal the SPD's uncertainty as to how to win that victory.

The Social-Democratic Party was a "revolutionary" party, for one thing, because it was committed to the achievement of "socialism." "Socialism" was an ill-defined concept—though perhaps not quite as ill-defined as it has become in the course of the twentieth century and especially since 1917—but it clearly suggested something very different from—indeed, in some ways the very opposite of—the prevailing order of "capitalism," and something that could not be attained by mere reforms. What the SPD sought, then—the change from capitalism to socialism—could be thought of as a social revolution. Referring to a change both drastic and far-reaching and necessarily gradual, the word "revolution" here has connotations similar to those in the term "industrial revolution."

To initiate the process of the social revolution, the Social-Democratic Party needed first of all to gain power. This, too, would involve a drastic but necessarily less gradual change, and the Party was hence committed not only to a social but also to a political "revolution." In the context of the German Empire, the SPD could hope to gain power only through a preceding or simultaneous process of democratization of the political order. The political revolution, to which the SPD was looking forward, then, amounted to the replacement of the imperial regime by a parliamentary democratic republic, such as was achieved in the Revolution of 1918–19.

In Marx's usage, too, the term "revolution" referred to both social and political revolutions. What is more, Marx did not consistently advocate or predict a particular form of political revolution. He was certain that the proletariat would have to come to power, but not whether it would do so suddenly or gradually, by violent or by peaceful means.[18] Thus, the SPD or at least the Marxists in it could adopt and employ the

Marxian concept of revolution with its certainty as to the outcome of the revolution and its uncertainty as to its form.

On the one hand, the SPD could not rule out the use of violence. Given its assumption of continuing growth of the labor movement, the persistence of bitter class conflict, and the stubborn resistance of the regime and its supporters to democratization and major pro-labor reforms, the occurrence of some kind of explosion in the future could not be ruled out. In particular, it was always possible that a regime founded on policies of "blood and iron," and fearful of a growing threat from labor, would resort to a coup d'état[19] or to violence to suppress labor organizations.

On the other hand, the German labor movement was obviously not a movement that hoped for, let alone planned, a violent revolution. Although its organizations encouraged and inspired intense loyalty and even discipline, they were open mass organizations, not secret conspiratorial ones that could have plotted insurrection or trained and armed their members for such purposes. A violent clash with the regime would have risked the very existence of these organizations that had been so successfully built up and that provided a sense of belonging and security for their members and a raison d'être for their sizable bureaucracies. Finally, the SPD's labor constituency, even if it was alienated, had made sufficient material progress, or could hope for it, to be unwilling to go to the barricades, especially when the prospects of success against a well-organized, well-armed regime enjoying the strong support of broad antilabor strata in the population were, to say the least, dubious.

In short, the SPD in imperial Germany could well think of itself as a revolutionary party. It was committed to make both the social revolution of introducing socialism and the political revolution of coming to power and introducing democracy, and it fully expected to do both—but, under the prevailing circumstances, it could not do so.

The Marxian concept of revolution was not only appropriate to describe the German Social Democrats' hopes and commitments along with their uncertainty, it also served some very useful functions for their movement. For one thing, the promise of ultimate success provided by its determinism justified their optimism in the face of what could well have been seen as a hopeless situation. That optimism was essential if the growth and elan of the movement were to be maintained. Though the labor movement provided important social, psychic, and material benefits to its members within the existing society, it would surely have lost much of its appeal had it proclaimed its great goals but admitted that it had no way of attaining them.

What made the great final goal of socialism so attractive, particularly to those deeply discontented in the existing society, was that it was radically different from the latter, and that was precisely what the word "revolution" suggested.[20] Commitment to a future society that, however vaguely, was expected to provide social justice and freedom, dignity and material abundance, could be a source of strength and pride, of solidarity and class consciousness for workers living in an environment of poverty and dirt, of repression and discrimination. It could even make those at the bottom of the social ladder feel morally superior to those at the top, who were seen as intent only on preserving and enhancing their privileges and their wealth. Since the goal of socialism was associated with and was attainable only through the socialist party and the other organizations of the labor movement, commitment to the goal became commitment to the Party and the movement and became a source of strength for them.

The use of the word "revolution" also strengthened the SPD more directly. In thinking of itself as a revolutionary party, the SPD drew a sharp line between itself and all other parties. In a multiparty system, it was not just one party among many; it was different from all others. They stood for the status quo or at most for mere reform; it stood for "revolution." Of course, the other parties and the regime saw the SPD in the same light, and this reinforced its self-image. Party leaders and Marxist ideologues feared that if differences between the SPD and other parties were blurred, if the Party watered down its "revolutionary" democratic and socialist principles, some of its adherents might defect. If their principal commitment was to democratization, they might vote for left Liberals or Progressives. If, on the other hand, especially in the early years, the SPD seemed insufficiently radical to them, they might be attracted to the anarchists or the anti-Semites.

At least the Marxists in the SPD felt that emphasis on its "revolutionary" character, then, would and should serve to keep the socialist labor movement sharply distinct and isolated from the rest of the political system, and thus internally integrated and unified. That emphasis both responded to and reinforced the isolation of labor from the rest of German society. In a situation in which the labor movement could not "make" a revolution (i.e., could not democratize the Empire and could not come to power), it could only hope and wait, without knowing exactly what it was hoping and waiting for. All it could do in the meantime was to prepare itself for the "revolution" by strengthening its organization, that is, by organizing its adherents and by attracting new ones, which in fact became its main task in the German Empire. To the extent that the concept of revolution helped in this process, it played an important role in the history of Social Democracy in that period.

There were certainly strong forces in the German socialist labor movement that shied away from the use of this concept. Some saw it as an obstacle to their goal of securing support from left-liberal circles in the bourgeoisie and the white-collar middle class. Some wanted to extend the appeal of the Social-Democratic Party to the peasantry and therefore needed to deemphasize and dilute its proletarian character.[21] To many holding leadership or administrative positions in various labor organizations, strengthening these organizations within the existing society—securing more members for them and more subscribers to their publications, more votes in elections and more seats in legislative bodies—either became virtually an end in itself or was seen as as means of securing reforms and concessions from the regime and from employers, a means of gradually "growing into" socialism without any revolutionary upheaval.

In view of the fact that the German Empire collapsed and the democratic revolution came in 1918 as a result, in the first instance, not of SPD pressure but of Germany's defeat in World War I, we cannot know whether Eduard Bernstein's optimistic expectation that socialism could be achieved in this nonrevolutionary way and his concomitant explicit demand that his party drop all of its revolutionary verbiage was justified.[22] That the Revisionist position could develop and had substantial support within the labor movement is certainly a symptom of the growing strength of that movement and of its increasing self-confidence. What needs to be emphasized in our context, however, is the powerful resistance to Revisionism within the Social-Democratic Party, for it indicates the deep attachment of many in it to Marxian conceptions. Since these included not just hidebound ideologues but also practical politicians, who had proved their ability to build and lead the movement in the real world of the German Empire—above all, August Bebel—it can be assumed that they appreciated the useful functions Marx's concepts served for their movement.[23]

Today, Bernstein's famous remark that the final goal of socialism meant nothing to him, but the movement everything,[24] may seem quite sensible. After all, we now know that the "final goal," as socialists conceived of it at the turn of the century, was never going to be reached, while the "movement" was destined to be remarkably successful in helping to make the industrial world a better one for workers. In this better world, socialist parties can now do without "socialism" to appeal to workers (and the many others whose votes they now need, given the shrinkage of the industrial working class). In the German Empire, however, where Bernstein's remark was made, it overlooked the distinct possibility that the labor movement, which meant so much to him, might have been unable to function effectively, or even to exist as it did, without the myth of the "final goal" of socialism to inspire it. As Victor Adler, the leader of the Austrian Social Democrats in the Habsburg monarchy and, like Bebel, a very realistic politician, said, "All our wearisome day-to-day work derives its sanctity and dignity from the value it has for the achievement of our final goals."[25]

Of course, faith in a socialist future was not necessarily associated with acceptance of Marxist theory. Many a German Social Democrat was deeply attached to that faith, yet was in no sense or only in a very superficial sense of the word a Marxist. Still, to the extent that a mass party with some diversity within it can be said to have had an official doctrine, that doctrine was Marxism, as it was expressed in the Social-Democratic Party's Erfurt Program of 1891, drafted by Kautsky with Engels's approval. Presumably such a program could not have been adopted, had Marxism not been widely regarded in the Party as serving its needs. As we have now seen, the position of labor in the German Empire gave key concepts in Marx's view of proletarian politics—class struggle and revolution—considerable relevance and hence great appeal.

SOCIAL DEMOCRACY SINCE 1918

The influence of Marxism in the German labor movement must be explained with reference to the peculiarities of the social and political system of the German Empire, where rapid industrialization took place under an aristocratic regime and aristocratic values were widely held in the population. Socialism and the revolution were, as Guenther Roth put it, "anti-ideals pitted against the official values of imperial Germany."[26] The failure of Marxism to gain much influence in the British labor movement suggests that had German society and government been more like British society and government, the influence of Marxism would have been correspondingly smaller.

My analysis of the appeal of Marxism in Germany thus necessarily had to concentrate on the period of the Empire. Once Marxist influence had become deeply rooted, however, it did not come to an end with the Empire. The Revolution of 1918–19 and the newly founded Weimar Republic changed some but not all of the conditions that had made Marxian concepts relevant and appealing. The agrarian and industrial upper classes that had dominated the Empire remained powerful not only in the economy but also in the government of the Weimar Republic, especially in its nonelective institutions of the bureaucracy, the military, and the judiciary. Hence the concept of class struggle continued to make sense and to be attractive to workers, and the SPD—I shall touch on the German Communists in chapter 4—continued to see itself as leading labor's class struggle.

Socialism and thus, at least by implication, the social revolution remained the final goal of Social Democracy. The goal of the political revolution, however—the establishment of a democratic republic, within which it could hope to come to power and to introduce socialism by electoral and parliamentary means—had been achieved in the Weimar Republic. Consequently, the SPD no longer saw itself as a revolutionary party and was no longer seen as an enemy of the existing political system. On the contrary, those who had—rightly—accused it of playing that role in the Empire now blamed it—again rightly—for being a pillar of the established republican system.

On the other hand, under the Nazi regime, when there was obviously no question, as there had been under the Empire, of Social Democrats advancing through reforms and trade union pressure, let alone through elections and parliamentarism, the concept of revolution was strongly revived in illegal and exile SPD thinking and writing. Revolution now meant not merely social revolution, and it did not mean a peaceful and more or less gradual conquest of power; it meant violent overthrow of the Nazi regime. As such, the concept may not have been relevant as a practical policy, for this kind of revolution was hardly possible, but it was certainly appealing to anti-Nazis to whom no channels of opposition were open.

It was, then, not until the post–World War II period that Marxism lost its relevance and appeal in Germany. Socialist ideologies and the socialist labor movement, and particularly Marxism, with its emphasis on class struggle and revolution, were reactions to the growth of capitalism in a deeply class-divided society, in which the aristocracy and its institutions and values were still powerful. The final destruction of the German and especially the Prussian aristocracy by World War II and the subsequent inclusion of its principal territorial base in the Soviet Union, Poland, and East Germany were, then, an important factor accounting for the decline of Marxist influence in Germany. Given the widespread identification of Marxism with Communism, and hence with the Soviet regime, fear and resentment of Soviet influence no doubt also contributed to this decline.

But other factors resulting from changes in the nature of the economy also worked strongly in this direction by tending to integrate the working class into the larger society. These factors include the acceptance of labor as a legitimate social partner and the extension of the welfare state and rising living standards for workers; the diversification of the working class into more numerous and more specialized occupations and skill levels, with the relative share of blue-collar workers and especially unskilled workers declining and that of service employees growing; resulting from these trends, a reduction in distinctions between workers and nonworkers; and an increase in the white-collar, salaried, new middle class, whose interests are not as sharply distinct from or opposed to those of labor as were those of the propertied old middle class of the petty bourgeoisie and the peasantry.

With workers no longer isolated and discriminated against, their unity and solidarity, their feeling of having common interests different from those of the rest of society, their class consciousness have declined and disappeared. It is now impossible for a socialist party to appeal to some perceived common interest that is specific to workers and that unites them. And with the proportion of labor in the population shrinking, it also is impossible for a socialist party to gain a majority of votes in national elections, as it had once expected to do, by appealing only to workers—even if it could mobilize the support of all workers, which itself is increasingly difficult.

On the other hand, a socialist party can now, with the growing heterogeneity of the middle class and the blurring of the line between it and the working class, extend its appeal to growing nonworking-class elements of the population and thus change from a working-class party to a "people's party." The SPD made that change explicitly in its Godesberg Program of 1959. That the Marxian doctrine and vocabulary, with their emphasis on class conflict and on the unique historical role of the proletariat, are inappropriate for such a party in the second half of the twentieth century is obvious. Nor are trade unions, representing a shrinking and increasingly heterogeneous working class, or socialist parties, now less dependent on and responsive to a laborite constituency than ever, likely to react to the erosion of labor's gains and status in recent years by a return to Marxism.

Chapter Three

The Evolution of Leninism

LENINISM AND MODERNIZING INTELLECTUALS IN UNDERDEVELOPED COUNTRIES

Lenin Reinterpreted

As Communist regimes in Eastern Europe and the Soviet Union have collapsed or crumbled, the historical role of Lenin and of Leninism has been widely reexamined and reevaluated. In this process, Lenin's image of himself as a Marxist thinker and as the leader of a proletarian movement and revolution has often been accepted as valid. In this essay, I reject this image and offer a more far-reaching reinterpretation of Lenin that presents him as one of the first ideologists of revolutionary modernizing movements in underdeveloped countries and as the leader of such a movement and its revolution in underdeveloped Russia.

Contrary to a now frequently expressed view, the collapse of Communist regimes is no evidence of the failure of Leninism. As an ideology of modernizing revolution, it inspired the group of modernizers who successfully seized power in the course of the Russian Revolution and some of whom then achieved the principal goal of the modernizing revolution, the rapid industrialization of their backward agrarian country. Thus, Leninism succeeded in the Soviet Union and also in those Balkan countries where Communist regimes were in their beginnings agents of revolutionary modernization. In the process, Leninists created industrial societies where Leninism is no longer relevant, and that is why it is now being questioned. They created bureaucratic structures that may have been functional for turning backward agrarian societies into industrial ones but have proved to be dysfunctional for organizing and running an advanced industrial economy. These structures could not meet the demands of consumers created by advanced industrialism, as Leninists had met the demands of intellectuals seeking rapid modernization.

Lenin successfully performed his historical role as a modernizing revolutionary in an underdeveloped country. Where he failed was in the role that he believed and claimed he was performing, that of a Marxist leader and theoretician. He failed as a Marxist political leader because he did not lead a mass working-class movement in a class struggle against capitalism that culminated in a revolution bringing the working-class movement to power; neither did he and his successors lead a government of workers governing in the interest of workers. All of which merely says that he failed to achieve what was impossible in underdeveloped Russia.

Lenin failed as a Marxist theoretician because he effectively rejected the basic assumptions of Marx's conception of history by substituting will power and organizational power for the development of the forces of production as the dynamic element in history. Thus, he believed that peasants, if properly led, could make the bourgeois revolution; that the Party could divert workers from their spontaneous trade unionist tendencies; and that the Party also could make a socialist revolution where there were few, if any, workers. I will note all this below and also show that Lenin's class analysis was often quite non-Marxian, particularly with respect to the peasantry.

In this chapter, I shall argue that Lenin failed as a Marxist because he was a successful revolutionary modernizer. In his policies, he responded effectively to the political reality of underdeveloped tsarist Russia. He recognized that the enemy he was fighting was not capitalism but the aristocratic-bureaucratic regime, that the Russian bourgeoisie was too weak to make a revolution, and that what little working class there was tended to become trade unionist rather than revolutionary. On the other hand, he saw the revolutionary potential of the huge peasantry and, above all, the key role of intellectuals in revolutionary politics.

All this is, of course, also to say that Lenin succeeded as a modernizing revolutionary because he failed as a Marxist; his policies did not rest on the Marxist ideas to which he believed he was devoted. According to these Marxist ideas, the bourgeoisie and the proletariat were the most powerful actors in modern politics; each was a revolutionary class in its time. Intellectuals, on the other hand, were assigned no independent role by Marx, and peasants were treated as a minor, contemptible remnant of the past.

One can be a successful revolutionary modernizer in an underdeveloped country or a Marxist, but one cannot be both at the same time.

Karl Marx's Marxism, after all, was obviously concerned with an industrial environment and appealed to labor movements in industrialized countries. It has no immediate relevance to modernizing movements in countries with little or no industry or industrial labor. Lenin merely employed Marxian concepts and, to make them relevant to the politics of underdevelopment, had to pervert their original meaning, as when he said that the bourgeois revolution would be made by peasants and the proletarian revolution by the Party.

If I present Lenin as using Marxian words to express an ideology quite different from Marxism, I am not suggesting that he was too naive, let alone too stupid, to understand Marxism or, on the other hand, that he knew very well that he was not a Marxist but cleverly pretended to be one by speaking Marx's language. Lenin was obviously not a stupid or a naive man but a sophisticated politician, and, equally obviously, he did not spend his entire adult life consciously pretending to be what he was not and filling what came to be some forty volumes of his collected works with deliberate lies. And even if Lenin had been naive or a liar, one can hardly assume the same of other Leninists, all those who surrounded and followed him and who adopted his Leninist ideology as well as his Marxist language.

I touch below on why Lenin and other Russian revolutionaries at the turn of the century were inclined to read Marxist literature and were attracted to the Marxist vocabulary, especially to the word "revolution." When they read their Marx and Engels and, until 1914, their Kautsky, some of them understood what they read in the light of their Russian experience and not in the light of those thinkers' Western European and German experience that had shaped their ideas. As practical revolutionary politicians, they were far more familiar with and passionately involved in the Russian than in the very different Western political environment, and it seems almost inevitable that, reacting to the former, they would misread the writings of thinkers reacting to the latter and take out of them or read into them what they needed, ignoring what did not fit their needs. Neither deceit nor stupidity need be assumed to explain this very common process.

Revolutionary Modernizing Intellectuals

I have sought to explain the development of Marxism with reference to the changing position of labor movements in the latter half of the nineteenth and the first half of the twentieth century in Western Europe and specifically in Germany. Similarly, I must now, in order to understand the development of Leninism in underdeveloped countries, briefly analyze the position of intellectuals in their political environment, for it is intellectuals who become the carriers of that ideology.[27] While German

Social Democracy was clearly the outstanding example of a labor movement influenced by Marxism, Leninism has had a powerful impact on
intellectuals in underdeveloped countries around the world, beginning
with Russia. I must therefore emphasize what intellectuals in such countries have in common rather than discuss their position in any one
country, such as Russia or China, Cuba or Ethiopia.

As one of the early consequences of commercial and colonial contacts
between industrialized and traditional agrarian societies, some aristocrats and merchants in the latter may send some of their sons to advanced countries for a higher education, typically to the advanced
country to which their own is linked, and eventually modern institutions
of higher education may be established in the underdeveloped country.
A small group of intellectuals is thus likely to emerge in such countries.

As a result of their exposure to the culture of industrial society and
to an education appropriate to such a society, natives of an underdeveloped country may acquire not only certain modern knowledge and
skills but also modern views and values. They may come to believe in
the benefits of material progress and of science and technology, in the
desirability of reducing social and economic inequality, in public policy
being legitimized only by the representation and even participation of
great masses of people in its formulation and execution—all values
widely accepted only as a result of industrialization.

What must strike natives of largely traditional societies exposed to
such values is their total irreconcilability with the status quo in their
own societies. Commonplace and generally shared as these values are
in industrialized societies, they are deeply subversive and revolutionary
in societies governed and exploited from time immemorial by a thin
stratum of aristocrats owning or controlling the land with its peasants
and by the traditional military, bureaucracy, and clergy employed or
formed by aristocrats and, in more recent times, sometimes also by a
colonial elite from abroad.

Obviously, the intellectuals I have in mind here do not include traditional ones, like Confucian or Islamic scholars, but even those with a
modern education absorb modern values to very different degrees. On
the other hand, these values can be acquired by means other than an
advanced modern education, particularly by service in the higher ranks
of modern armies and bureaucracies, institutions that may be introduced
even in industrially quite backward countries by their ruling aristocracies
or colonial powers. In underdeveloped countries, then, intellectuals, as
I use that word, are defined with reference not to their education but
to their modern values, interests, and attitudes; they can well be called
modernizers or modernizing intellectuals.

Modern values being revolutionary in nonmodern societies, those
committed to them in such societies are revolutionaries. For one thing,

they stand for a social revolution, for, in order to realize their values, they want to convert the traditional agrarian order into a modern industrial one. Having seen the latter and regarding, in its light, the former as wholly intolerable, they want to bring about the change as rapidly as possible.

Unwilling to have the industrial revolution in their countries progress as gradually as it did in the West, modernizing intellectuals want to force its pace, which can be done only by far-reaching government intervention in the economy. Since neither traditional aristocrats nor colonial governments can be expected to undermine the bases of their own existence in the agrarian and colonial economy, the modernizers must take over the government themselves. They are thus not merely social but also political revolutionaries, and they will want to use their governmental power to mobilize and allocate resources of labor and capital to advance industrialization. Both to pursue that goal and to attack their aristocratic and colonial adversaries, they will take such measures as the expropriation of landed estates (often called land reform) and the nationalization of colonial industry, such as mines and railroads (often called socialism).

Given their belief in equality, progress, and mass representation, intellectuals think of themselves as representing the poverty-stricken masses. In agrarian countries, these are overwhelmingly peasants, though they may include a small minority of workers where industrialization has set in, particularly in its colonial form of the development of extractive industries (e.g., mining and plantations) and of means of transportation (e.g., railroads and ports). The intellectuals' attitude toward these masses is typically ambivalent. On the one hand, they idealize and glorify them as those who ought to, and eventually will, rule and those whose interests they, the intellectuals, serve and seek to advance.

On the other hand, intellectuals are impatient with and distrustful of the masses, because they are difficult to mobilize for the revolutionary cause. Peasants, after all, having lived from time immemorial in an unchanging environment, in ignorance, and in the isolation of their villages, tend to be politically passive and, in this sense, conservative, even if they are deeply discontented. Even workers, who have recently been torn out of this environment, may express their resentment of their new urban and industrial setting by wishing to return to their peasant existence and, in any case, being miserably poor, are more likely to be concerned with immediate improvements of their situation than with visions of a new and different society under their own domination.

Still, modernizers may look to workers even more than to peasants for mass support, because workers are more accessible to them and more easily organized, and they may be more open to promises of change and to anticolonial views as they face colonial employers. Also, modernizing intellectuals often think of themselves as socialists, partly because they favor the nationalization of industry and sometimes of land, and partly because their teachers and models in advanced countries are much more likely to have been on the (anticolonial) Left than on the (pro-colonial) Right. As socialists, intellectuals have learned from the West, they must have a labor following.

Along with modern views and values, Western-educated intellectuals acquire the vocabulary associated with Western politics and particularly with whatever Western ideology they adopt. They thus come to think of politics in their own underdeveloped countries in terms of concepts that acquired their meaning from the politics of industrialized countries and hence may be more or less irrelevant in their own environment. If they act in line with the original meaning of these concepts, they are likely to fail politically. If they succeed politically, it is because they have infused a new meaning appropriate to their nonindustrial environment into the "industrial" concepts, but they do retain the old terminology.

This has been the fate of words like "nationalism," "socialism," and "democracy." Nationalism changed from an ideology advocating that people speaking a single language be united in a single state into a quite different ideology seeking to unite people, regardless of their language and ethnicity, against the political and economic manifestations of colonialism. Socialism changed from an ideology advocating equality and power for an industrial working class to a quite different one advocating industrialization under the leadership of intellectuals acting through their government. Democracy, linked in Europe to representative parliamentary government with universal suffrage and civil liberties, has in underdeveloped countries lost all meaning except that of a vague claim, available to any leader, movement, or regime, that he, she, or it represents the "people."

The word "Marxism" has undergone a similar change of meaning from the social theory formulated by Karl Marx and Friedrich Engels to something vaguely incorporating the meanings of what "nationalism," "socialism," and "democracy" stand for in underdeveloped countries. But here it is not just a single word being retained. A whole conceptual vocabulary of words—"capitalism" and "socialism," "bourgeoisie" and "proletariat," "class struggle" and "revolution"—had to be retained by those who considered themselves "Marxists." Yet in its original meaning, that vocabulary did not fit the social facts they confronted; it therefore had to be watered down or changed in its meaning.

As intellectuals employ Western concepts, these concepts become myths that, once accepted by them and often also by their opponents, affect political behavior no matter how irrelevant their original meaning may be in their new environment. If a politician in an underdeveloped country calls himself a socialist or a Marxist, his policies will evoke reactions, friendly and hostile, at home and abroad that they might not evoke if he used a different label, and he in turn will respond to these reactions.

Political processes putting an end to traditional aristocratic and colonial regimes have, more or less clearly, occurred in virtually all underdeveloped countries. It is a striking fact that in spite of numerous cultural and historical differences among such countries and in spite of the small numbers of modernizing intellectuals, they have played a key role in these processes and generally been overrepresented, at least in the first generation of leaders forming the successor regimes in most underdeveloped countries.

This is not to deny major differences in the role of the intellectuals in different countries. Thus, in independent countries like Russia and Ethiopia, they see the domestic traditional ruling groups as their principal enemies, while in colonies like India and Indonesia, their main drive is directed at the colonial power. Still, they all seem to share the twin goals of industrialization and independence, though some may emphasize the former and some the latter.

In some cases, as those of the Chinese Communists and the Algerian nationalists, modernizing intellectuals could mobilize a large mass following in their quest for power; in others, such as in the Egyptian and Libyan revolutions, a relatively few army officers could remove and replace the old regime. That difference is, of course, related to that between protracted guerrilla warfare and a quick coup d'état, just two of various forms—peaceful or violent, gradual or sudden—that revolutions of modernizers can assume.

The new modernizing leaders also differ widely with respect to their success in realizing their goal of rapid and far-reaching industrialization. The new Soviet regime, enjoying a head start as a result of the industrialization introduced in the final decades of tsarism, turned a backward country into a major industrial power; the Chinese Communists and the newly independent Indian government, too, had great measures of success; other modernizing regimes were less successful, and some failed totally. Successful industrialization leads to the replacement of revolutionary modernizing intellectuals as leaders by new technocratic and managerial bureaucrats. Failure may lead to an antimodern reaction, such as religious fundamentalism, or to continuing conflicts among modernizing intellectuals, who blame each other for the failure and who may mobilize other groups that may come to replace those in power.

Immense as all these differences are, we need not be concerned with them here, for our interest is not in the general course of political change in underdeveloped countries but in the appeal of "Marxism-Leninism" to some of their intellectuals.

THE APPEAL OF LENINISM

From Proletarian Revolution to Modernizing Revolution

A doctrine as centrally concerned with capitalist industry and the industrial working class as Marxism is obviously irrelevant in countries without or virtually without capitalist industry or an industrial working class. It is not Marxism, then, that has appealed to intellectuals in underdeveloped countries but another ideology that retained the Marxist promise of a successful revolution. It is very appealing to such intellectuals and extremely relevant in traditional and colonial societies under the impact of modernization.

The revolution, however, now had to be divorced from the working class, and hence from the very foundation of Marx's promise. He and his followers in the Western socialist parties had never predicted or advocated just any kind of revolution. It is of the essence of the Marxian system of thought that capitalism turns the industrial proletariat into a revolutionary class and makes its eventual victory inevitable. Advocates of any kind of revolution other than a proletarian one against capitalism (or, at an earlier stage of historical development, of a bourgeois one against feudalism) cannot rely on Marx for support. Marx was not an analyst or an advocate of revolutions of one ethnic group against another, of intellectuals against colonialism, of peasants against landlords, even of the "masses," the "toilers," or the "poor" against the rich and powerful.

In Marx, the two themes of the advancement of the working class and of revolution are inextricably linked. The working class cannot advance beyond a certain point without winning its revolution, and the revolution is necessarily a proletarian revolution, that is, it is fought by the proletariat and brings the proletariat to power. In the course of the development of Marxism, the advancement of labor became the real content of its program and policies, while revolution, as we saw in chapter 2, gradually changed from a predicted event to a myth that gradually lost its power to inspire behavior, until the theme of revolution disappeared altogether.

It could be argued that in underdeveloped countries, the fate of the two Marxian themes was simply reversed. It was revolution that was the real content of the programs and policies of movements that thought of themselves as Marxist, while the theme of the advancement of the working class soon became a myth to be eventually dropped. It must be stressed, however, that the two themes are not equally essential in Marx's theory. A movement adhering only to the laborite theme can retain its Marxian character, while a movement adhering only to the revolutionary theme is not Marxist, as I have defined that term.

The advancement of labor from a state of poverty, impotence, and degradation to one of prosperity, power, and dignity is at the very heart of Marx's thought. If "revolution" merely means the conquest of power by labor, then the revolutionary theme is as essential as that of the advancement of labor, simply because it is part of it. But if the theme of revolution refers to a more or less sudden and violent event replacing a government, as it has in underdeveloped countries, then that theme is a less essential component of Marx's thought than that of the advancement of labor and is separable from his theory.

In the West, it took the better part of a century for the theme of revolution to become wholly separated from that of the advancement of labor and to disappear as the environment of the labor movement changed so as to make the concept of revolution more and more inappropriate and irrelevant. In underdeveloped countries, too, what in the young Lenin could still be seen as the Marxian doctrine had to travel through some time and, even more, through some space for the two themes to become separated, a process in which the laborite essence of Marxism was lost and a different ideology that still retained Marxist terminology arose.

To the extent that the two processes of the two Marxian themes becoming separated are similar, one can see tsarist Russia playing a role similar to that of the German Empire. The labor movement in the present Federal Republic of Germany would have paid little more attention to Marx's thought than did the British labor movement, if in its century-long history from Karl Marx to Willy Brandt there had not been for nearly half a century the German Empire, whose authoritarian government and repressive and discriminatory labor policies kept the concept of revolution alive at least as a relevant myth. Similarly, revolutionary modernizing intellectuals in countries like Ethiopia and Afghanistan would have paid no attention to what Marx wrote about capitalism long ago and would not have claimed to represent an actually nonexistent working class, if between Marx and Mengistu and Najibullah there had not been Lenin, who employed the language of Marx with its proletarian emphasis, and the Russian Revolution, which was described in Marxian terms and in which real workers played a significant role.

The German Social-Democratic Party, from its beginnings to the present, has maintained its concern with the advancement of labor and thus could (if it were so inclined) claim a certain continuity in its history going back, in part, to Marx, precisely because, in the period of the Empire, Marx's other theme of revolution also remained relevant. Similarly, revolutionaries in underdeveloped countries can—wrongly, in my view— see themselves as descendants of Marx, because in Lenin and the Russian Revolution not only the theme of revolution but also that of the advancement of labor retained some relevance.

In this sense, then, turn-of-the-century Russia served a function similar to that of the German Empire, as the former was the locus of the replacement of Marxism by Leninism and the latter produced the transmutation of Marxism into modern Social Democracy. To be sure, the industrial proletariat in Russia constituted only a small fraction of the total population, not remotely close to the proletarian majority Marx had in mind when he thought of the revolution. Also, it consisted mostly not of workers matured, experienced, and united in the course of long class struggles, as Marx imagined his proletariat, but of peasants recently displaced into industry and discontented and even revolutionary for that very reason. Still, there were workers in the final decades of the tsarist empire, and, when Lenin thought and wrote of proletarians and even of revolutionary proletarians, he was not referring to a mere fiction.[28]

It was surely the theme of revolution that attracted Lenin, a revolutionary intellectual, to Marxism,[29] and the existence of real workers in Russia no doubt helped to make Marx's concept of proletarian revolution appear relevant to Lenin's needs. Thus, Lenin came to think, speak, and write the language of Marxism, a language appropriate to industrialized societies, just as many intellectuals in underdeveloped countries have come to adopt the languages of ideologies of industrialized societies.

As Lenin functioned as an effective revolutionary politician in an underdeveloped country, the concept of revolution came more and more to be divorced from the proletariat in his thought, his policies, and, as I shall note, even in his language. It was Lenin's intellectual-led revolution, as distinguished from Marx's proletarian revolution, that could appeal to some other modernizing revolutionary intellectuals in underdeveloped countries, even if it remained clothed in the inappropriate language of Marxism.[30]

Indeed, the Marxian language lent to the prediction and advocacy of revolution a scientific character that impressed intellectuals in underdeveloped countries inclined to admire Western science. Like Lenin himself, they were attracted to the prospect and the scientific promise of revolution, and they could accept the Russian Revolution as a model along with the Marxian socialist and proletarian language that Lenin and his successors had attached to it. They might even use the term "proletarian revolution" for the revolution they hoped to and sometimes did make, but in their practice that revolution had few, if any, links to any real proletariat, which may not even have existed in their underdeveloped countries.

For Marx, the revolution would not be a result of revolutionary ideas held by intellectuals like himself, but a reaction of the proletariat to its changing position in capitalist society. When Marx and Engels wrote in one of their early works that "the existence of revolutionary ideas in a particular period presupposes the existence of a revolutionary class,"[31] they were merely saying what was obvious from the perspective of their conception of history. Social classes, rooted in relations of production, are in the base of the historical process; ideas and ideologies are in the superstructure; and it is changes in the base that "in the last analysis" determine changes in the superstructure, not vice versa.

Thus, it could never have occurred to Marx and Engels, two intellectuals with revolutionary ideas, to search for a revolutionary class. To them, that class was given, and their own revolutionary ideas were merely a consequence of its existence. Similarly, their followers in the next generation, who became leaders and ideologists of the newly emerging socialist parties in Central and Western Europe, took it for granted that support for their ideas would come primarily from industrial workers. This expectation, even if it was to some extent self-fulfilling, was powerfully reinforced when it proved to be largely accurate. Marxist leaders and Marxist ideology were accepted by political parties associated with labor movements, and it was workers—though by no means all workers or only workers—who provided what mass support they enjoyed. Clearly, for Marxists in industrialized Europe, there was no problem finding and identifying a revolutionary class or, rather, *the* revolutionary class; as Marx and Engels had said, their ideas, that is, their very existence as Marxists, presupposed the existence of such a class.

For Lenin and Leninists in underdeveloped countries, on the other hand, finding a revolutionary class is a very serious problem; indeed, it is an insoluble one. Revolutionary modernizing intellectuals in underdeveloped countries derive their ideas from industrialized countries. If such ideas are to be thought of as superstructural, their base is to be found abroad. Revolutionary ideology in India or Russia may rest on a base in Britain or Germany, not in India or Russia. Thus, it is quite possible for modernizing intellectuals in an underdeveloped country to hold a revolutionary ideology even though there is no revolutionary class in their country. For many, this presents no problem; they may be able to mobilize support from various discontented groups or even to make their revolution by themselves, particularly if they control the military. But Lenin and Leninists, thinking only in terms of the Marxian conceptual vocabulary, felt obliged to associate their revolutionary ideology with a revolutionary class. The search for such a class was a major, perennial preoccupation for Lenin.

For Marx, in industrial Europe, the answer to the question of what class would make the next revolution seemed so simple and obvious as to render the question superfluous. Lenin in underdeveloped Russia, and then his followers in other underdeveloped countries, on the other hand, debated endlessly whether the next revolution would be bourgeois or proletarian, or perhaps a little bit of both, or begin as one and end as the other. They worried about the roles the bourgeoisie and the proletariat would play in this revolution, for it could not be assumed that the bourgeoisie would be revolutionary in the bourgeois revolution or even that the proletariat would make—initiate and lead—the proletarian revolution. And, more relevant in underdeveloped countries, what role would the peasantry play in the bourgeois and/or proletarian revolution? Was it more bourgeois or more proletarian, or perhaps petty-bourgeois or semi-proletarian?

Given the political situation they confronted in their underdeveloped countries, Lenin and his followers could never come up with definite and consistent answers to such questions. As I hope to show in some of the following pages, Lenin was, in spite of his vocabulary and because of his realism, unable to think of politics clearly in terms of classes and of class conflict. No doubt, this is one major reason why Leninism, in contrast to Marxism, proved to be relevant to the needs of revolutionary modernizers.

Industrialization

I must now try to explain the appeal of Leninism to modernizing intellectuals in underdeveloped countries and the character of Leninism as a response to the sociopolitical environment of traditional agrarian societies under the impact of modernization coming from industrialized societies. If one defines an ideology with reference to the social groups whose interests it represents and to whom it appeals, then, to make the argument persuasive that the ideology propounded by Lenin was a modernizing one, it must be shown that his thought represented the interests of and appealed to modernizing intellectuals, that the relevant attitudes characteristic of modernizing intellectuals were also held by Lenin.

The implications of Lenin's thought and its differences from Marxism have become clearer in the thought, and especially in the political practice, of Leninist leaders in the underdeveloped world in recent decades than they were in Lenin's own thought and behavior, because Lenin was so much closer to Marx both temporally and geographically than they are, and because turn-of-the-century Russia was industrially more developed than are their countries. If I can show that even the European Lenin, born in Marx's lifetime, replaced Marxism with an ideology fitting the needs of modernizing intellectuals in underdeveloped countries, that Lenin was a Leninist and not a Marxist, it will be obvious that those in Asia, Africa, and Latin America who think of themselves as "Marxists-

Leninists" a century after Marx adhere to the Leninist rather than the Marxist ideology, and that it is Leninism and not Marxism that has had some appeal and has survived in underdeveloped countries.

I must, then, turn to some of the elements in Lenin's thought, in addition to the most obvious one of revolution, that could appeal to the intellectuals whose values, goals, and attitudes I briefly described above. It will be immediately apparent that none of these elements are present or well developed in Marx's thought. Rather, they all constitute additions to or modifications of Marx's Marxism, and some are incompatible with it.

Having adopted Western industrial values, modernizing intellectuals commonly feel ashamed of the backwardness of their countries and bemoan what they regard as their inferiority vis-à-vis the advanced industrialized countries. This was a common theme in the thought of intellectuals in pre-Revolutionary Russia and is pervasive in Lenin's writings, where he frequently deals with the backwardness of the Russian peasantry and sees the solution to the problem in rapid industrialization.[32]

Until 1914, Lenin still shared the Marxian assumption that industrialization would have to be, and would be, brought about by capitalism, which, he thought, in Russia would require a political revolution to turn peasants into landowners and into a new bourgeoisie, as the existing one was tied to the tsarist autocracy.[33] During World War I and especially during the Revolution, Lenin decided that there was no need for capitalism any more, but that industrialization could be advanced through government control if the government, in turn, was controlled by the Party, which he sometimes simply identified with "the workers."[34]

It was this non-Marxian idea that became a key element of Leninism and that proved attractive to modernizing intellectuals who were intent on the rapid industrialization of their underdeveloped countries and for whom the capitalist route to industrialization that Marx had envisaged seemed neither available nor desirable. Nor did Lenin's naiveté and ignorance regarding industrialization[35] shock them, for these characteristics were similar to their own; the first generation of modernizing intellectuals in underdeveloped countries were typically trained as lawyers (like Lenin), physicians, teachers, or journalists rather than as economists, scientists, or engineers. Like Lenin, they had little understanding of but great faith in Western science and technology.

Lenin expressed this faith when he said *"Communism is Soviet power plus the electrification of the whole country.* . . . Only when the country has been electrified, and industry, agriculture and transport have been placed on the technical basis of modern large-scale industry, only then shall we be fully victorious."[36] In his last article, he wrote, "we [have] to develop our large-scale machine industry, to develop electrification, the hydraulic extraction of peat . . . etc. In this, and in this alone, lies our hope."[37]

It was principally only after Lenin's death, under Stalin's rule, that industrialization was, in fact, undertaken by the Soviet regime.[38] In recent years it became quite evident that the Soviet economy, as it was built up and directed under Stalin, could not meet the demands for consumer goods of broad strata in a now industrial society. But that should not obscure the relevance and attractiveness of Soviet industrialization to modernizing intellectuals, who did not live in industrial societies or worry about their problems, but were eager to create such societies.

Stalinist industrialization, as it is foreshadowed in Lenin's thought, was appealing to such intellectuals because it was rapid and emphasized heavy industry as the basis of further industrialization, it was carried out largely independent of Western capital, and it was directed by intellectuals and created new opportunities for them. Above all, it was successful in attaining the goal of modernizing intellectuals of turning a backward agrarian society into a modern industrial one. The huge price paid for this success in terms of many millions of people being deprived both of material welfare and of freedom of movement, of choice, and of expression could easily be ignored by modernizing intellectuals and may not have seemed so great to them in the context of the widespread material and intellectual poverty in their own countries and in relation to the hoped-for rewards to be obtained at this price.

Anti-imperialism

The emphasis in Lenin's thought—and in Stalin's practice—given to rapid industrialization that proved so appealing to modernizing intellectuals in underdeveloped countries was a reaction to the fact that in the early twentieth century Russia itself was still a largely underdeveloped country. To put it briefly, Lenin's thought has appealed to modernizing intellectuals because Lenin was himself a modernizing intellectual.

Lenin shared, however, the then widespread misconception, to which I shall return in chapter 5, that the modernizing revolutionary movements of Russia and Eastern Europe were part of the international labor movement. As a result, he saw himself not only as functioning in his own underdeveloped country but was also concerned with the politics of Western industrialized countries and especially with their labor movements, though he had little understanding of them. When, during World War I, they behaved in ways incompatible with his conception of Marxism, he developed his theory of imperialism as a necessary stage of capitalism.

In this theory, Lenin was intent on explaining the War as an imperialist one and thus on justifying his wartime policy of revolutionary defeatism and on denouncing Social Democrats who opposed that policy, whether they supported or opposed their belligerent governments. He was not particularly interested in the effects of imperialism on underdeveloped countries. Tsarist Russia was in Lenin's view one of the imperialist powers, even if the weakest link in the chain of imperialism, rather than a victim of imperialism. He therefore did not think of his revolutionary struggle as one to liberate his country from the oppression of foreign imperialist enemies.

After the Revolution, however, Lenin identified his regime or at least saw it as allied with the victims of imperialism. In 1919, he declared: "It is self-evident that this revolutionary movement of the peoples of the East can now develop effectively, can reach a successful issue, only in direct association with the revolutionary struggle of our Soviet Republic against international imperialism."[39] And in his last article, "Better Fewer, But Better," Lenin bluntly spoke of the coming "conflict between the counter-revolutionary imperialist West and the revolutionary and nationalist East,"[40] and by implication identified his own revolution with the "nationalist," anti-imperialist one.

Lenin's thought on imperialism has been powerfully appealing to modernizing intellectuals who see themselves as engaged in a struggle with imperialism. Feeling that their countries have been exploited and kept backward and dependent by the colonial policies of industrialized powers, they find an explanation in Lenin's theory. Often they come to regard imperialism as representing all the complex forces opposing them and obstructing the attainment of their goals, as the single enemy so useful in politics.

The fact that Lenin's theory links imperialism inextricably to capitalism also appeals to modernizing intellectuals, who often oppose capitalism. They may do so because some native capitalists in their society can be closely linked to the colonial economy. Other capitalists, though, may suffer from it and be potential anticolonial allies of the modernizers; and in any case, native capitalists are not a major political force in underdeveloped countries. The intellectuals' opposition to capitalism is more likely to be due mainly to the anticommercial prejudices of the aristocratic culture in which they grew up and to the attitudes they absorbed from their Western teachers and models.

The modernizers' anticapitalism, which, as anti-imperialism, is concerned with the colonial impact on the economy of the underdeveloped country, is quite different in its motivation and its policy content from Marx's laborite anticapitalism, just as nationalization of the means of production to advance industrialization of an agrarian economy is quite different in form and content from Marx's socialization designed to uplift workers and to abolish social classes. But the words and symbols of anticapitalism and socialism have been employed by both Leninist modernizers and Marxist labor movements, allowing the former to think of themselves as "Marxists-Leninists" or simply Marxists.

Intellectuals and Workers

Leninist ideologists and leaders in underdeveloped countries have been mostly intellectuals, but so have the ideologists of Marxism and many leaders of Marxist parties in industrial countries. The leading role of intellectuals in itself does not, then, distinguish Leninism from Marxism. However, intellectuals in the two different environments have different values and interests, and this essay is concerned with the values and interests that ideologies express and with the groups associated with these interests. Leninism expresses values and interests of modernizing intellectuals; Marxists, even if they are intellectuals, represent workers' interests.

Leninists stand for rapid industrialization of their societies, both because they see it as bringing progress to these backward societies and because, like most people, they think a good society is one in which people of their own kind play an important role, as intellectuals expect to do in the process of industrialization and in an industrialized society. If and when they do industrialize, modernizing intellectuals or their managerial successors are quite willing to let the price of that costly process be paid in good part by workers in terms of their material standard of living and of their individual freedom. Marxist intellectuals, on the other hand, operating in already industrialized countries, favor greater material and cultural benefits and more power for workers. What may well be the outstanding example of a government controlled by a Marxist party for a considerable period of time, the Social-Democratic municipal government of Vienna in the 1920s and early 1930s, built extensive public housing. Leninists built steel mills.

While Marxist leaders and ideologists were intellectuals, they were not, like Leninists, modernizing intellectuals. Certainly they were in favor of modernity; they accepted industrialism and did not wish to solve its problems by a return to the simpler agrarian society. The workers they wanted to represent were, after all, a product of industrialization; and more industry would be needed to produce more workers and more wealth and to lay the basis of the future socialist society that would provide abundance for all.

The creation of industry, however, was, according to Marx, the historical function of capitalism. It was to be accomplished by the bourgeoisie before its domination was ended by the victory of the labor movement, which could itself only be a response to capitalist industry. To the generation of Marxists after Marx, this must have seemed like an obvious truth, for they saw capitalist industry and a socialist labor movement growing up all around them. Marxists, then, did not think it was the task of their movement to bring about industrialization, because it was already being brought about by capitalism. They did not expect to come to power until industrialization was far advanced. They thought that they were close to this point in Germany and Austria and that Britain, too, was near a labor victory. Where industry was not advanced, as in Russia and Italy, they called for patience with respect to the socialist revolution. Thus, as I will note in chapter 4, the Mensheviks argued that the revolution due in Russia was the bourgeois one.

The Marxists were proved wrong in their assumption, derived from Western experience and generally shared in their day, that industry could be created only by capitalism. Leninists, especially and first in Russia, proved that modernizers, too, can industrialize. But the point here is that Leninists wanted to, and did, assume responsibility for modernization; Marxists did not. Leninists were modernizers; Marxists were not.

Probably the most obvious reason why Leninism appeals to intellectuals is that it is an ideology that assigns a key role in the modernizing revolution to intellectuals. It does so because it is itself a response to the process of modernization and thus recognizes that intellectuals play a key role in it. What makes this less than obvious is merely the fact that in expressing his ideology, Lenin employs the language of Marxism, a different ideology concerned with the different historical process of the development of capitalism and of the proletarian revolution, in which it assigns a key role to the industrial proletariat.

Thus, Lenin thought of his modernizing revolution as a proletarian revolution and of workers playing the leading role in the revolutionary movement. They do so, however, as represented by intellectuals or, as Lenin put it more often, by his Party or simply by "us." The introduction of "the Party" is generally seen as Lenin's major modification of or contribution to Marxism, but it does not merely add an organizational element that was absent in Marx's Marxism. Marx's social-democratic successors had added such an element long before Lenin did, but it continued to express Marx's concern with the working class. The introduction of Lenin's "party of a new type" involves a change of the ideology from a laborite ideology to one of intellectuals. The Party is, and "we" are, in Lenin's mind clearly distinct from the working class and must lead that class where it would otherwise not go. In short, it is intellectuals, not workers, who give direction to and lead the revolutionary movement.[41]

As much as Lenin changed his position on other issues, he remained very consistent on the leading role of the Party, that is, of intellectuals. Here it will suffice if we document this with two well-known passages from *What Is to Be Done?*, his principal work on the subject. There he argued that workers, by their own efforts, can develop only trade union consciousness, but that "Social-Democratic consciousness . . . would have to be brought to them from without . . . by intellectuals." What is more,

the spontaneous working-class movement is trade-unionism, . . . and trade-unionism means the ideological enslavement of the workers by the bourgeoisie. Hence our task, the task of Social-Democracy, is *to combat spontaneity, to divert* the working-class movement from this spontaneous trade-unionist striving to come under the wing of the bourgeoisie, and to bring it under the wing of revolutionary Social-Democracy.[42]

I noted earlier that modernizing intellectuals typically have an ambivalent attitude toward the small working class of their underdeveloped countries. This is clearly true of Lenin as well. On the one hand, like anyone who thought of himself as a Marxist in his day, he ascribes to the working class the central role in contemporary and future history. On the other hand, he obviously doubts that it can play that role. As the passages just quoted indicate, he views workers with considerable disdain and distrust. A year before he wrote these passages, he expressed that disdain for workers not led by his Party of intellectuals when he wrote: "Isolated from Social-Democracy, the working-class movement becomes petty and inevitably becomes bourgeois."[43]

Peasants and Peasant Revolution

The modernizing intellectuals' attitude toward the far more numerous peasantry is politically much more important than their attitude toward the working class. It, too, is likely to be ambivalent, and that was also true of Lenin's attitude. Just as the proletariat could be trusted only as long as it was led by the Party, that is, by modernizing intellectuals, so the proletariat was to lead the peasantry,[44] meaning that, directly or indirectly, intellectuals must lead the peasantry, too.

By and large, before the Revolution of 1905, Lenin thought of the peasantry as a dying class that would become proletarianized under inevitably coming capitalism, and he therefore favored "class struggle in the countryside."[45] Even during the 1905 Revolution, he predicted a "new class struggle between the peasant bourgeoisie and the rural proletariat"—two class categories quite alien to Marxism, which does not confuse industrial and preindustrial classes—and he noted that "the peasantry includes a great number of semi-proletarian as well as petty-bourgeois elements." He even predicted that in the future "the proletariat must accomplish the socialist revolution, allying to itself the mass of the semi-proletarian elements of the population, so as to crush the bourgeoisie's resistance by force and paralyse the instability of the peasantry and the petty bourgeoisie."[46] This would seem to say that the semi-proletarian peasants are to paralyze the instability of the peasants.

At the same time, Lenin expressed his contempt for the peasantry when, outlining the "major social forces," he described it as follows: "The petty-bourgeois and peasant section. Tens of millions. The 'people' *par excellence*. Greatest state of benightedness and disorganization . . . they have most to gain *directly* from the revolution. The greatest instability (today—for the revolution, tomorrow—for 'law and order' after slight improvements)."[47] Lenin was not always sure, then, whether the peasantry—or its semi-proletarian component—could be an ally of the proletariat, nor did he clearly indicate whether it could serve as such only in the bourgeois revolution or also in the future socialist one, when he distinguished between these two at all. But he certainly came to see the revolutionary potential of the peasantry in 1905.

Caught up in his Marxian categories, Lenin was emphatic that the 1905 Revolution could not be proletarian and socialist, but only bourgeois and capitalist. He stressed that "the immediate and complete emancipation of the working class [was] impossible. Only the most ignorant people can close their eyes to the bourgeois nature of the democratic revolution which is now taking place." It "will, for the first time, really clear the ground for a wide and rapid, European and not Asiatic, development of capitalism; [and] will, for the first time, make it possible for the bourgeoisie to rule as a class."[48]

But in the same pamphlet of 1905, "Two Tactics of Social-Democracy in the Democratic Revolution," in which he insisted on what in Marxian language he called the bourgeois character of the revolution, Lenin stressed that this revolution was made not by and for the bourgeoisie, but by the proletariat and especially by the peasantry: "the bourgeoisie is incapable of carrying through the democratic revolution to its consummation, while the peasantry is capable of doing so."[49]

Without . . . becoming socialist, or ceasing to be petty-bourgeois, the peasantry is capable of becoming a wholehearted and most radical adherent of the democratic revolution. The peasantry will inevitably become such if only the course of revolutionary events, which brings it enlightenment, is not prematurely cut short by the treachery of the bourgeoisie and the defeat of the proletariat.[50]

Only the proletariat can be a consistent fighter for democracy. It can become a victorious fighter for democracy only if the peasant masses join its revolutionary struggle. If the proletariat is not strong enough for this, the bourgeoisie will be at the head of the democratic revolution and will impart an inconsistent and self-seeking nature to it. Nothing but a revolutionary-democratic dictatorship of the proletariat and the peasantry can prevent this.[51]

Looking back on the 1905 Revolution some two years later, Lenin was quite clear on the agrarian content of that "bourgeois" revolution. He referred to "the peasant revolution as one of the varieties of bourgeois revolution" and to "the concept of peasant bourgeois revolution,"[52] and stated that "every peasant revolution directed against medievalism, when the whole of the social economy is of a capitalist nature, is a bourgeois revolution."[53] He concluded that

the agrarian question is the basis of the bourgeois revolution in Russia and determines the specific national character of this revolution. The essence of this question is the struggle of the peasantry to abolish landlordism and the survival of serfdom in the agricultural system of Russia and, consequently, also in all her social and political institutions.[54]

Lenin could, then, at least verbally have his Marxian cake of the bourgeois revolution and eat it, too, in an underdeveloped country without a revolutionary bourgeoisie and with a potentially revolutionary peasantry. Taken literally, the idea of a bourgeois revolution, "at the head" of which must not be the bourgeoisie—a bourgeois revolution that is not made by the bourgeoisie but by peasants led by workers, that is betrayed by the bourgeoisie, and that brings to power not the bourgeoisie to develop capitalism but a presumably anticapitalist "revolutionary-democratic dictatorship of the proletariat and the peasantry"—certainly is, from a Marxian perspective, nonsense. But while Lenin's thought as a social theorist was fatally flawed by his application of Marx's concepts to an environment quite different from Marx's, he did not let these concepts interfere with the pursuit of policies he considered appropriate to his underdeveloped Russian environment.

Lenin's bourgeois revolution is a peasant revolution or, as he puts it, again having his cake and eating it, too, a "peasant bourgeois revolution"; but the peasants must be led by the workers, who, in turn, must be led by the Party of intellectuals. It is, incidentally, because Lenin expects his Party, which he sometimes identified with "the" workers, to lead both the proletariat and the peasantry that he does not have to explain why the far more numerous peasants would accept the leadership of the workers. In short, Lenin's bourgeois revolution turns out to be the revolution of modernizing intellectuals mobilizing what mass support they can among the lower classes, that is, mostly the peasantry. Marx's view of class struggle, revolutions, and historical stages derived from the experience of industrial Western Europe is replaced by a very different view relevant to the experience of underdeveloped countries but confusingly expressed in the Marxian vocabulary.

Marx and Lenin on Bourgeois, Proletarian, and Peasant Revolutions

In Marx's theory, the bourgeois revolution against feudalism and the proletarian revolution against capitalism are sharply distinct and separated by a considerable period of time. The conditions for the proletarian revolution—the growth of industry and of the proletariat—are created only in this period of the bourgeoisie's predominance following its revolutionary victory. In Lenin's thought, the "bourgeois" revolution that results in the dictatorship of the proletariat and the peasantry is not clearly distinguishable from the proletarian revolution that results in a similar dictatorship. The two revolutions merge into one that is, in fact, neither bourgeois nor proletarian, but is the revolution of modernizing intellectuals. As Lenin, somewhat like Trotsky at the time, wrote during the 1905 Revolution: "from the democratic revolution we shall at once . . . begin to pass to the socialist revolution. We stand for uninterrupted revolution."[55] His failure to think clearly in terms of two distinct revolutions no doubt accounts for Lenin's indecisiveness as to the difference, if any, in the peasantry's role in the two revolutions.

When Lenin saw his opportunity to seize power in Russia in November 1917, he effectively decided—in the face of opposition from those of his followers who saw this as a startling innovation—to skip the bourgeois revolution altogether and to move directly to what he thought of as a socialist revolution, and his new revolutionary government claimed to represent both workers and peasants.[56] Looking back on his revolution two years later, he clearly saw it as a revolution of both workers and peasants against both capitalism and feudalism:

In our struggle against feudal survivals and capitalism, we succeeded in uniting the peasants and workers of Russia; and it was because the peasants and workers united against capitalism and feudalism that our victory was so easy. . . . The Russian revolution showed how the proletarians, after defeating capitalism and uniting with the vast diffuse mass of working peasants, rose up victoriously against medieval oppression.[57]

The Marxian scheme of two revolutions with an intervening period of growing capitalism and a growing proletariat did not fit the needs of Lenin as a modernizing revolutionary in an underdeveloped country. Such revolutionaries look forward to the one revolution that will put an end to the old regime and bring them to power to modernize their country. Like Lenin, many of them call their revolutions "socialist," often because that word links them to Marx and always because it vaguely promises a better future, especially for the lower classes. But such "socialist" revolutions in underdeveloped countries, beginning with the Russian one, were not and could not be made by labor movements, nor did they or could they bring them to power.

Concern with workers and appeals to them by modernizing intellectuals, especially those, like Lenin, in the early twentieth century, may be due to Marx's influence and also that of the German Social-Democratic Party, then regarded as the model Marxist party. In an underdeveloped environment, depending on whether the working-class segment of the population was small, tiny, or nonexistent, these appeals and concerns were more or less irrelevant politically. On the other hand, appeals to and concern with the peasantry as a major ally were a response to the environment rather than to Marxist or SPD influence.

Marx, with French peasants in mind, called the peasantry "the class which represents barbarism within civilization,"[58] hardly a way to describe a revolutionary ally of the proletariat. The hammer and sickle would have struck him as a strange symbol for a revolutionary proletarian party. The SPD, though it could have benefited from peasants' votes, refused and was unable to make an effective appeal to them, because their interests clashed with those of its prime constituency, the working class. Marx and the SPD, obviously, responded to conditions in France and Germany;[59] Lenin responded to conditions in turn-of-the-century Russia.

Just as he had done in shifting the leading role in the revolutionary movement from the proletariat to the intellectuals, so in recognizing the potential of the peasantry as a revolutionary ally, Lenin took account of the reality of the underdeveloped environment in which he operated and implicitly acknowledged the irrelevance of Marxism to it. He continued to speak of the proletariat and the bourgeoisie, but, as an effective revolutionary politician, he recognized the key role of intellectuals and peasants in the revolutionary politics of underdeveloped countries. He saw that the bourgeoisie and the proletariat were weak and would not make revolutions, and, while retaining their class designations, he substituted the peasants and the intellectuals for them.

By referring to the peasants as a "rural proletariat" and as "semi-proletarian," Lenin obfuscated the difference between what to Marx was a remnant of the preindustrial order without a revolutionary role in capitalist society and the industrial working class whose strength and revolutionary class consciousness would inevitably grow with the growth of capitalist industry. The tremendous emphasis in Lenin's thought on the peasantry, like that on the Party, that is, on modernizing intellectuals—both elements quite absent in Marx's thought—make Lenin's Leninism relevant to conditions of underdevelopment and the needs of modernizing intellectuals, and hence are major factors accounting for the appeal of Leninism to the latter.[60]

That Lenin was realistic in putting the peasantry in a central position in his revolutionary scheme is shown by the fact that what mass support Leninists have actually mobilized in underdeveloped countries has been drawn largely from the peasantry, not only in Russia but also notably in China and Vietnam. Although peasants can, then, be far more numerous supporters of Leninist-led movements and revolutions than intellectuals and can be crucial for their success, I have emphasized the latter here because it is they, beginning with Lenin, who became Leninists.

Peasants—and the same is probably true of workers—are not likely to be caught up in the Leninist ideology. They do not favor the rapid industrialization of their societies independent of foreign capitalism and therefore mostly at the peasants' and workers' expense. Whatever it is, other than Leninism, that may motivate them to support Leninist-led movements and sometimes to take great risks on their behalf cannot—and need not—be adequately dealt with in an essay on Leninist ideology.

No Class Struggle in Russia

In making intellectuals the leaders and peasants the principal allies or, indeed, components of the revolutionary movement, Lenin implicitly recognized that that movement was not Marx's proletarian movement born of the class struggle against capitalism. It was, rather, a modernizing revolutionary movement directed against the traditional aristocratic order and—less in Russia than in many other underdeveloped countries—against foreign colonialism. In Lenin's day, it was, to be sure, not possible for him and his contemporaries to see, let alone explicitly to describe, the situation from this point of view, which has become much more accessible to post–World War II generations. This is a matter I will touch on in chapter 5.

Modernizing revolutionary movements in underdeveloped countries are not class movements fighting a class struggle. Some modernizing intellectuals do not even seek support beyond their own ranks of students and professionals, including modern army officers. If they do, they can, with more or less success, turn to all kinds of people who, torn out of their traditional passivity and impotence by the beginnings of modernization, have grievances against the traditional aristocracy of big landlords, the clergy, bureaucrats, and army officers. Supporters of the modernizers may be recruited both from modern strata, like the intelligentsia, workers, and what "bourgeoisie" of businessmen there might be, and from traditional strata, like peasants and small traders and artisans. In opposition to colonialism, they may even be joined by elements from the traditional aristocracy.

The concept of class struggle that is central to Marxism, both that of aristocracy versus bourgeoisie and that of bourgeoisie versus proletariat, is largely irrelevant in the politics of modernizing movements in under-developed countries fighting traditionalism and colonialism. Obviously this is particularly true if there is hardly any bourgeoisie or proletariat in these countries. In turn-of-the-century Russia, a bourgeoisie and a proletariat did exist, and Lenin was much too deeply influenced by Marx not to think of the political conflicts he was engaged in as class struggles. Nevertheless, his thought undermines the Marxian concept of class struggle and is, for that very reason, relevant to the needs of modernizing intellectuals and appealing to them.

For one thing, there is, derived from his theory of imperialism, Lenin's theory of "combined development" of the two major Marxian class strug-gles, of the bourgeois-democratic and the proletarian-socialist revolu-tions proceeding simultaneously in underdeveloped countries. It legitimizes all sorts of alliance strategies combining and cutting across Marxian class categories as well as reliance by modernizing revolution-aries on support from various groups.[61]

The theory of combined development is still expressed in terms of classes and class struggles, but the implications of Lenin's thought are destructive of these Marxian concepts. If it is intellectuals, organized in the Party, that must lead the revolutionary movement, these intellectuals need not confine their following to workers. The Party can turn to other classes for support, to add them to or even to replace the working class.[62] It can appeal to all kinds of people who, if they join the Party, will, by definition, be referred to as proletarians and, if they follow the Party, will be accepted as allies of the proletariat. In fact, they all constitute a modernizing movement.

This logic of Leninism has become quite manifest in so-called Marxist-Leninist movements in underdeveloped countries in recent decades, as I shall note when I turn to these movements, but to a considerable extent it was made explicit already by Lenin himself. Most obviously, Lenin added peasants to workers as being mobilizable on behalf of his revo-lutionary movement. But he also blurred and watered down the concepts of classes, as Marx had defined them, as he adjusted to the reality of Russian politics and, in particular, to the revolutions of 1905 and 1917.

We have already seen how unclear Lenin's conceptions of the peas-antry and the bourgeoisie were, and I will note in a moment that this was even more true of his thinking with respect to underdeveloped countries other than Russia. More and more the proletariat, too, came to be expanded in his mind beyond industrial workers and to be replaced by wider and looser categories like the "masses" and the "toilers."[63]

Marx, in an industrial environment, could imagine that the proletariat was or soon would be the great majority of the population. For Lenin, in underdeveloped Russia, similarly to claim that his ideology repre-sented the interests of a vast majority, the peasants had to be combined with the workers in some non-Marxian category.[64] In March 1917, he wrote that "the Soviet of Workers' Deputies is an organisation of the workers, the embryo of a workers' government, the representative of the interests of the entire mass of the *poor* section of the population, i.e., of nine-tenths of the population."[65] Here Lenin conceives of workers as representing all the poor, regardless of their class—that is, virtually the entire, in fact still overwhelmingly agrarian, population of Russia.

But even before 1905, Lenin had stressed that his Party had to appeal to all classes, especially in *What is to Be Done?* That this emphasis is to be found in his principal early work on the role of the Party suggests that Lenin's "classless" approach is, indeed, linked to his conception of the leading role of intellectuals. This becomes evident when he writes: "*We* must take upon ourselves the task of organising an all-round political struggle under the leadership of *our* Party in such a manner as to make it possible for all oppositional strata to render their fullest support to the struggle and to our Party."[66]

"The Social-Democrats must *go among all classes of the population*; they must dispatch units of their army *in all directions.*" "We must have 'our own people,' Social-Democrats, everywhere, among all social strata." Lenin precedes both these sentences with statements saying this was necessary "to bring political knowledge to the *workers,*" but the second one is followed immediately by the statement that "such people are required, not only for propaganda and agitation, but in still larger measure for organisation."[67]

On the next page of *What Is to Be Done?*, Lenin states very bluntly that

our task is to utilise every manifestation of discontent, and to gather and turn to the best account every protest, however small. . . . Indeed, is there a single social class in which there are no individuals, groups, or circles that are discontented with the lack of rights and with tyranny and, therefore, accessible to the propaganda of Social-Democrats as the spokesmen of the most pressing general democratic needs?

This is followed by a reference to Social-Democratic political agitation "among *all* classes and strata of the population" and the statement "that in order to become the vanguard [of the revolutionary forces], we must attract other classes."[68]

No Class Struggle in the "East"

If Lenin advocated the inclusion in the revolutionary movement of people, regardless of their class, in Russia, thus implicitly seeing his country as an underdeveloped one, where Marx's concept of class struggle did not apply, it is not surprising that he did the same with respect to even less developed countries.

After Lenin had been in power for about two years, his hopes for Communist revolutions in Central and Western Europe began to fade. These hopes had rested on the false assumption that underdeveloped Russia and a revolution there could serve as a model for industrialized countries. He now became interested in seeing in underdeveloped countries revolutionary prospects and possible allies for his own new revolutionary regime in Russia and he began to emphasize the relevance and possible appeal of the new Soviet experience to potential revolutionaries there.[69] He generally refers to underdeveloped countries vaguely as "the East," and thinks principally of Asia, for Africa south of the Sahara and Latin America evidently remained terrae incognitae for Lenin throughout his life.

Lenin now speaks of "the revolutionary masses of those countries where there is no proletariat or hardly any,"[70] and by demanding the unity of these "masses" with "the revolutionary proletarians of the capitalist, advanced countries,"[71] he calls attention to their nonproletarian character. He refers to them by such vague terms as "the toiling masses," the "working masses," "the whole mass of the working population,"[72] "the oppressed masses of the colonial, Eastern countries,"[73] and "the oppressed masses, those who are exploited, not only by merchant capital but also by the feudalists."[74]

What Lenin advocates in his statements to the Second Congress of the Communist International of July–August 1920, from which these phrases are quoted, is "the closest alliance with Soviet Russia of all the national and colonial liberation movements . . . of the bourgeois-democratic liberation movement of the workers and peasants in backward countries or among backward nationalities,"[75] and "the closest possible alliance between the West-European communist proletariat and the revolutionary peasant movement in the East, in the colonies, and in the backward countries generally."[76]

Yielding to the objections of the Indian delegate, M. N. Roy, who evidently found it more difficult than did Lenin to accept the idea of Communist "active assistance" to and an "alliance" with a "bourgeois" movement,[77] Lenin agreed to substitute the term "national-revolutionary" movement for "bourgeois-democratic" movement in the final report to the Congress. But in noting this, he immediately added that "it is beyond doubt that any national movement can only be a bourgeois-democratic movement, since the overwhelming mass of the population in the backward countries consists of peasants who represent bourgeois-capitalist relationships"[78]—though a page and a half later he also referred to "peasant feudal and semi-feudal relations."

It is quite clear, then, that Lenin expected the revolutionary movement in underdeveloped countries, as in Russia, to include peasants—indeed, no doubt, to consist mostly of peasants as well as, more generally, of the "masses"—even where, as he says, there are no proletarians.[79] Whether Lenin also sought to appeal to the bourgeoisie in underdeveloped countries and perhaps thought that the "masses" and especially the "bourgeois-democratic" movement would be led by members of the bourgeoisie is less clear.

Though he had severed Marx's immediate link between the revolution and the working class either by inserting the Party between the two or even by substituting it for the working class, Lenin was still too wedded to Marxian conceptions to be able to conceive of revolutions as anything other than either bourgeois or proletarian. Still reluctant to designate revolutions in countries without a proletariat as proletarian, he had to identify them as bourgeois. Thus, paradoxically, it is peasants and even workers, or at least their political and economic roles, that are described as bourgeois, as when, in the passages just quoted, peasants are said to represent "bourgeois-capitalist relationships" and "the bourgeois-democratic liberation movement" is described as a movement "of workers and peasants in backward countries." Lenin can, then, in the same breath, urge Communists to "assist" this "bourgeois" movement and speak of "the struggle against the bourgeoisie" and "victory over the bourgeoisie."[80]

But if workers and peasants are "bourgeois," what about the bourgeoisie? Is it "bourgeois" or anti-bourgeois? What is its role as a class vis-à-vis the "bourgeois-democratic movement" that is fighting "against the bourgeoisie"? Here Lenin is, not surprisingly, ambiguous when he states that "the bourgeoisie of the oppressed countries, while it does support the national movement, is in full accord with the imperialist bourgeoisie, i.e., joins forces with it against all revolutionary movements and revolutionary classes."[81]

A number of factors may help to account for all this confusion as to who is "bourgeois." Generally, it results from the application of Marx's Western "industrial" vocabulary, the only one with which Lenin was familiar, to nonindustrial societies. More specifically, for one thing, Lenin, as a practical politician, recognized the key role of members of the privileged classes, like himself, in the revolutionary politics of underdeveloped countries. For another thing, he both used the Marxian term "bourgeoisie" quite loosely, where it had nothing to do with capitalism, and assumed, as a Marxian reflex, that his own revolutionary struggle was necessarily one against the bourgeoisie, even in countries where there was virtually no proletariat and virtually no bourgeoisie. Finally, the ambiguous and even self-contradictory last sentence quoted may be the result of an attempt to compromise with M. N. Roy on Communist policy vis-à-vis "bourgeois-democratic" movements in underdeveloped countries.

Lenin also seems quite confused or inconsistent regarding the peasantry. In Marx's conception of history, based on his understanding of the history of industrial countries, peasants do not play an important active role in the proletarian class struggle and revolution against capitalism. Lenin, concerned with agrarian countries, beginning with Russia, could not ignore or downgrade them as easily as Marx, but he was unable to think in terms of concepts and categories other than Marx's. This probably accounts for his difficulty in maintaining a consistent characterization of the peasantry. As we have seen, he referred to a "peasant bourgeoisie" and a "rural proletariat"; he called peasants "petty-bourgeois" and "semi-proletarian," and included them in the "toiling masses"; he said peasants represented "working people," "bourgeois-capitalist relationships," and "feudal and semi-feudal relations."

All this vagueness and ambiguity, confusion and inconsistency in Lenin's language regarding the class character of revolutionary movements in underdeveloped countries casts considerable doubt on his competence as a Marxist theorist, but, then, he would hardly have been taken seriously as such had he not been a successful revolutionary.[82] In that latter capacity, however, he did not really think in terms of classes—which accounts for his careless use of language—when it came to the question of who could be mobilized to join revolutionary movements. To the realist Lenin, everyone was welcome, regardless of class, who was willing to accept the leadership of the Party or could be useful to it.

The Party, nevertheless, remains in Lenin's eyes a workers' party. It is that regardless of whether workers are to be found, in whatever numbers, in its leadership or its membership, because it is intellectuals organized in the Party who represent proletarian class consciousness and, hence, the workers' "true" interests. The Leninist Party, then, is a workers' party by definition, and that is true even in societies where there are no workers.[83] Lenin, like all later Communists, often uses the term "workers" or "proletariat" as a synonym for the Party.

The Marxian class designations "proletariat" and "working class" remain prominent in the Leninist vocabulary, then, but they do not clearly refer to an actual social class and particularly the class of industrial workers, as they did in the usage of Marx and his followers in the West, whose parties relied on the support of real industrial workers. The linkage between the words and the class becomes more and more tenuous as Leninism moves from Russia to more underdeveloped countries.

Leninist Voluntarism and Marxist Determinism

Without becoming involved in the philosophical complexities of questions of determinism and free will, I might note that there is a distinct voluntarist flavor to Leninism that is another element shared by the thought of Lenin and that of other modernizing intellectuals and makes Leninism attractive to the latter. Like other such elements, this voluntarism stands in sharp contrast to Marxist determinism.

Thus, Marx and his social-democratic followers assumed that workers would quite naturally become class conscious, and therefore socialist, as a response to their position in capitalist industry and society. Lenin, on the other hand, insisted, as he was quoted above, that social democracy had "to combat spontaneity, to divert the working-class movement from this spontaneous trade-unionist striving to come under the wing of the bourgeoisie, and to bring it under the wing of revolutionary Social-Democracy." He even felt that peasants could be mobilized to support his revolution and then his Soviet regime.

Similarly, in the Marxist conception of history it is obvious that stages of historical development cannot be skipped, simply because the foundations of each stage are created only by the preceding stage. In particular, the advanced industry and mature mass proletariat that make socialism possible and, indeed, inevitable, are created only in the bourgeois capitalist stage of history. The socialist society could be built only on the technical and cultural achievements of the bourgeois epoch, for which Marx had great admiration.

Lenin, on the other hand, having long insisted on the necessity of a "bourgeois-democratic" revolution—though one to be made by the peasantry rather than the bourgeoisie—and thus on the necessity of a capitalist stage in Russia, once in power proceeded immediately to institute what he considered the socialist stage of history. His Soviet government was to—and under Stalin did—create the industry and the proletariat that, according to Marx, were a prerequisite of the socialist revolution and of socialism. As modernizers often see it, the old order of autocracy and imperialism was simply evil and had to be destroyed; the new order would not grow out of it but was to be built from scratch.

To both the problems of diverting workers from their spontaneous pro-bourgeois strivings and of creating socialism before its prerequisites existed, Lenin's solution was to rely on political will, organization, and leadership rather than on economic change. While the contrast between Marxist economic determinism and Leninist voluntarism can be sharply drawn, then, it also can be argued that Lenin's emphasis on will and organization, that is, on the role and very existence of his Party, were themselves "ultimately" economically determined. After all, almost any new political phenomenon in history can be traced back to some earlier economic change, if the analyst is inclined to explain it in this fashion and if, as an economic determinist, he or she will search no further once some economic causation has been found.

The difference between Marxist determinism and Leninist voluntarism can, then, perhaps be better described, and certainly can be better explained, as a difference between the conviction that victory is inevitable because economic development must necessarily produce the conditions of victory, and the conviction that victory is inevitable because the will to victory, whether it is economically determined or not, is invincible.

When history seems to be moving in the direction one desires, it is emotionally satisfying to think of its evolution as inevitable. Karl Marx saw the growth of industry and of an industrial working class in England in his lifetime and, not unreasonably, projected these trends as inevitable into the future. The next generation of social democrats witnessed the impressive rapid growth of labor movements and socialist parties, most notably in Germany, and of parliamentary democracy in Western Europe. They could reason that the inevitable growth of industry would inevitably produce a mass proletariat that would inevitably become socialist and, in a socialist party, would inevitably come to power.

Revolutionary modernizing intellectuals in underdeveloped countries, like Lenin, cannot rely on the visible historical dynamic of industrial and working-class growth to inspire their optimistic expectation of an inevitable victory. Their own numbers and organization are small and not necessarily growing; they often operate underground or in exile. The working class in their countries is either nonexistent or very small and ideologically still close to the peasantry from which it emerged only recently. And the peasantry, the great majority of the population, confined in the isolation of its villages, is overwhelmingly politically passive and ignorant, unorganized and unorganizable. On the other hand, traditionalist regimes of overlapping landowning, military, bureaucratic, and clerical elites that persisted through centuries and were never shaken by challenges from the lower classes, as well as colonial regimes with their great economic and military might, appear as quite powerful antagonists. Revolutionary modernizers cannot reasonably rely on inevitable historical trends to bring them to power and their hopes to fruition.

In underdeveloped countries there may not be much economic development, and what there is offers no obvious promise of inevitable victory to modernizing intellectuals. On the contrary, they may feel that they must first win their victory and come to power in order to initiate or speed economic development. Under such circumstances, revolutionary modernizers must count on their will power rather than on economic change to bring about the political changes they desire.

Karl Marx thus summarized his conception of history: "The mode of production of material life conditions the process of social, political and intellectual life in general. It is not the consciousness of men that determines their existence, but, on the contrary, their social existence that determines their consciousness."[84] The German Social Democrats' Erfurt Program of 1891 repeatedly employed the term "necessity" and one of Karl Kautsky's favorite words, *Naturnotwendigkeit*, meaning the necessity of nature or natural necessity, to explain how economic development must produce social change and a socialist labor party.[85]

On the other hand, modernizers like Mao and Castro, as Stuart Schram says of the former, "approach problems of every sort, including economic development . . . with . . . a conviction that he who is resolute and fearless must ultimately prevail."[86] As Mao wrote in one of his poems, "Under this heaven nothing is difficult, if only there is the will to ascend,"[87] and in an editorial, "Under the leadership of the Communist Party, as long as there are people, every kind of miracle can be performed."[88] Castro's speeches are full of phrases suggesting that "nothing can subdue or deter the will of the people."[89] In chapter 4, I will quote Antonio Gramsci as saying in so many words that men adapt brute economic facts to their will, and "will becomes the motor of the economy, the shaper of objective reality."

Lenin's voluntarism with its emphasis on the will, organization, and leadership of a few determined intellectuals shaping history was a response to the situation he faced in Russia, and as such was relevant to similar situations in other underdeveloped countries.[90] Clearly, it could be powerfully appealing to other revolutionary modernizing intellectuals, while the Marxist reliance on economic forces shaping the will and the actions of men could not inspire them.

LENINISM SINCE LENIN

From Mao to Mengistu

When Lenin was concerned with Russia, as he was in most of his thought, and much as he emphasized the peasantry, he could still refer to real workers, different as they were in numbers and character from those Marx had had in mind. Even when, in the 1920s, Li Li-san and M. N. Roy insisted that the proletariat was the leading revolutionary class, they could still point to real workers in China and India, although these constituted a tiny proportion of the population of their overwhelmingly agrarian countries and a tiny proportion of Communist Party members.

Within two or three years after Lenin's death in 1924, Mao broke the remaining link of Leninism with an actual working class by relying on an exclusively peasant mass base in rural areas of China.[91] One striking passage from Mao's famous Hunan Report suffices to illustrate his oft-repeated emphasis on the revolutionary potential of the peasantry and particularly of the poor peasantry:

This leadership of the poor peasants is absolutely necessary. Without the poor peasants there can be no revolution. To reject them is to reject the revolution. To attack them is to attack the revolution. Their general direction of the revolution has never been wrong.[92]

To be sure, the substitution by the Communist Party, that is, the intellectual leadership of the modernizing revolutionary movement, of a peasant following for a proletarian following can be partly obscured by calling the Party "the working class" and by referring to the peasantry or the poor peasantry, as Lenin had already done, as a "rural proletariat." The Marxian term "proletariat" is thus retained, but it is deprived of its Marxian meaning, for Marx had assigned a key role in history to industrial workers, not because they were, like peasants, poor and oppressed but because of their central role in industry.[93]

During the war with Japan, Mao expanded the range of classes that his Party claimed to represent by adding to the proletariat and to the peasantry not only the petty bourgeoisie but also the "national bourgeoisie" to form his "bloc of four classes."[94] The inclusion of the "anti-imperialist" bourgeoisie in this bloc is significant in our context, not because it might attract capitalists to join the Communist Party,[95] but because, once the Party sees itself as the representative of both the proletariat and the bourgeoisie, it effectively recognizes that the Marxian class struggle is not central in the politics of underdeveloped countries[96] and opens the door to the inclusion of people in the revolutionary movement without regard to class.[97]

The Maoist approach of mobilizing the broadest possible range of supporters against the Japanese invaders of China was also appropriate to Soviet needs in the period of the Cold War, and hence to Soviet-guided Communist parties throughout the underdeveloped world. This was proclaimed when the Soviet-sponsored World Federation of Trade Unions held a conference in Peking in November 1949. Here Liu Shao-chi declared the "Chinese path" to be obligatory for the Communist parties of underdeveloped countries and defined it primarily as one in which "the working class must unite with all the other classes, political parties and groups, organizations and individuals who are willing to oppose the oppression of imperialism and its lackeys."[98] This formula, at the time endlessly repeated in Communist policy statements throughout the underdeveloped world, seems to go as far as possible in obliterating the class character of the Communist party, telling "the working class," that is, the Communist parties, to unite with "all" classes.

This united front of all classes, now advocated from Moscow as well as Peking, was different from earlier ones, in which the Communist party, claiming to represent workers and also peasants, sought agreements "from above" with "bourgeois" parties, as in the periods of Chinese Communist collaboration with the Kuomintang and, primarily in Europe, of the Popular Front of the 1930s and the National Front of World War II. Now the Communist parties, in opposition to "bourgeois" parties, appealed "from below" directly to, and sought to unite with, the bourgeoisie and its individual members and claimed to represent their interests and, indeed, those of all classes. The Communist party became the party of the exploiters as well as of the exploited.

This shift in the Communists' conception of the nature of their parties could be documented at great length with quotations from Communist writings in the 1950s,[99] but this is not the place to do so. Nor is it necessary to trace the development of Leninist ideology beyond the point it had reached at midcentury[100] in order to show that it is an ideology appropriate to revolutionary anticolonial movements in underdeveloped countries rather than to labor movements in industrialized countries.

I may just note that in the course of the 1950s Communist parties in underdeveloped countries moved, under Soviet pressure responding to the Cold War, from opposition to support of the governments of their "neutralist" countries, governments of non-Leninist modernizing movements that Lenin used to call "bourgeois-democratic." Effectively, they gave up on "revolution," as they had earlier on "class struggle,"—or, rather, the revolution they now desired was not the one that would bring the Communist party to power, but the modernizing, anticolonial revolution that had in most cases already taken place.

There were even suggestions from Moscow that underdeveloped countries could evolve along "socialist" lines under the leadership of their existing modernizing regimes. Here I will quote only Nikita Khrushchev himself. When he visited Nasser's Egypt in May 1964, he repeatedly referred to it as "embarked upon the road of socialist development." Half a year earlier, in response to questions posed by Algerian, Ghanaian, and Burmese newspapers, he endorsed "socialism of the national type" and praised "revolutionary-democratic statesmen" who "sincerely advocate non-capitalist methods for the solution of national problems and declare their determination to build socialism. We welcome their declarations."[101]

More generally, in the early 1960s, Communist parties were urged to subordinate themselves to what were then called regimes of "national democracy," defined as anti-imperialist regimes led by "bourgeois" nationalists, that is, to the major non-Leninist modernizing movements. Communist parties and trade unions even came to merge with, and be submerged by, those of non-Communist revolutionary regimes, like Castro's in Cuba,[102] Nasser's in Egypt, and Ben Bella's in Algeria. Single parties of such regimes in Ghana, Guinea, and Mali were recognized as quasi or substitute Communist parties, for example, by having their delegates attend the Soviet Communist Party Congress of 1961.[103] In more recent years, single parties and their regimes that have no historic links with Communism at all, like those of Ethiopia and some other African countries, have called themselves Marxist-Leninist.

The Blurring of Leninism

That the bourgeoisie could lead a society to socialism would have struck Marx and even Lenin as utter nonsense. And Lenin would have been shocked by Communist parties giving up their independence. His draft statement to the Second Congress of the Communist International stressed that "the Communist International must enter into a temporary alliance with bourgeois democracy in the colonial and backward countries, but should not merge with it, and should under all circumstances uphold the independence of the proletarian movement even if it is in its most embryonic form."[104] Still, the startlingly un-Marxian directive of 1949 to Communist parties to unite with all classes merely repeats almost verbatim Lenin's demand in his *What Is to Be Done?* of 1902, quoted above, that, for purposes of agitation and organization, Social Democrats must "go among all classes of the population" and "among all classes and strata of the population," and must appeal to "individuals, groups, or circles" in all social classes.

Lenin, under the influence of West European culture and politics, especially of Marx's thought, and operating in a country in the early stages of industrialization, could not and did not need to develop Leninism consistently as an ideology of modernizing intellectuals in underdeveloped countries. It took a few more decades and the development of some tiny and some eventually powerful Communist parties in underdeveloped countries for Leninism to emerge in full bloom as an ideology of modernizing movements. The character of Leninism as such an ideology was now more and more confirmed both by Leninist Communist parties becoming like, supporting, and even merging with non-Communist modernizing movements and by some of the latter thinking of themselves as Leninist. The distinction between Communist and non-Communist modernizing movements became less and less clear, even where it persisted on an organizational level.

If the relevant implications of Lenin's thought did not become fully apparent until Leninism moved from Russia into even more underdeveloped countries, it is still clear that the crucial elements shared by the ideologies of modernizing, anticolonial movements are present in Lenin's thought. These are the hope for revolution with its twin goals of rapid, noncapitalist industrialization and of anti-imperialism; the insistence on the central role of intellectuals in the revolutionary movement, and the concomitant disregard of class and class struggle in the formation of this movement; the emphasis on the importance of including the peasantry in the movement; and an ambivalent attitude toward both workers and peasants as admirable yet not trustworthy allies. Lenin shared all these views with intellectuals leading modernizing movements—and none of them with Marx and Marxists.

Leninism, then, can be seen as one ideology in the broad category of ideologies of antitraditional and anticolonial movements in underdeveloped countries that are characterized by these views. It used to be distinguished from other ideologies in this broad category by its employment of the language of Karl Marx and by its association with Communist parties. Both of these distinguishing characteristics of Leninism, significant as they were in Lenin's own eyes, have gradually been eroded.

As to Marxian terminology, I have already noted how the term "revolution"—never an exclusively Marxian one in any case—was retained as highly relevant to the needs of revolutionary intellectuals in underdeveloped countries. But it referred no longer, as it had for Marx, to the culmination of the proletarian class struggle; rather, it referred to the victory of the modernizing movement, a revolution by now associated with the past as much as with the future.

The concepts of class and class struggle, without which Marx's Marxism is unthinkable, have more or less vanished from the thought and vocabulary of Leninism as have both the contestants of Marx's class struggle. The proletariat was replaced by "the masses" already in Lenin's own thinking about underdeveloped countries and has since tended to be merged in the even less Marxian category of "the people." The bourgeoisie, too, has tended to disappear, partly when its members (if there are any), comprised in "the people," participate in the modernizing movement, and partly because Marx's domestic "capitalism" has been replaced by Lenin's foreign "imperialism" as the enemy.

While Leninists, beginning with Lenin, changed the language of Marxism to adapt it to the political reality of underdeveloped countries, non-Leninist modernizing intellectuals, responding to the same reality, have employed much the same language. They, too, think of themselves and their policies as "revolutionary"; they, too, glorify and claim to represent the "masses"; and, above all, they, too, define their chief enemy as "imperialism." When Kwame Nkrumah entitled one of his books *Neo-Colonialism, the Last Stage of Imperialism*, he obviously had Lenin's *Imperialism, the Highest Stage of Capitalism* in mind. Other modernizing intellectuals, for example, Sukarno, have spoken and written as Leninists had come to speak and write, simply because their ideologies were similar or identical. The language of Leninism is no longer distinguishable from the language of modernizing movements in general, because the ideology of Leninism is no longer distinguishable from other ideologies of modernizing movements.

The link between Leninism and Communist parties, too, has, at least since the mid-twentieth century, been broken. In countries where the struggle against the forces of traditionalism and/or colonialism has been largely won, Leninism as an ideology of that struggle has become irrelevant, the more so the more industrialization has advanced. Communist parties in such countries do not necessarily disappear, but they are no longer led by or represent revolutionary intellectuals, and they no longer stand for what Leninism stood for, though they may long retain the language of Leninism, that is, the modified language of Marx.

This is true of Communist parties in power and out of power. Among the latter, the parties in Chile, Greece, Spain, and Portugal (relevant here to the extent that traditional elements remained strong in these countries in recent decades) and the two Communist parties of India represent various interests in their now more or less modernized societies, but they are no longer part of a modernizing movement and hence no longer Leninist.

The ruling Communist parties of China, North Korea, and the Soviet Union, of Poland, Hungary, and Yugoslavia, of Romania and Bulgaria were themselves more or less responsible for turning their underdeveloped countries into modern ones and thus rendering Leninism obsolete. They, too, came to represent interests characteristic of modern societies, largely those of the bureaucracy and technocracy; but even where their rule has not collapsed, as it has more or less in Eastern Europe and in some of the successor states to the Soviet Union, and still seems secure, as in China and North Korea, they are no longer Leninist.

On the other hand, modernizing ideology is alive and well where intellectual-led modernizing movements still perceive threats from traditional and/or colonial forces and where industrialization has barely begun or has not advanced successfully—but it is not necessarily Leninism or identified with Communist parties. In the few corners of the world where significant elements of traditionalism, like big landownership or strong monarchical institutions, still persist or where colonialism is still influential and where these are fought by modernizing movements—as in the Philippines and Nepal, in Guatemala and El Salvador—Leninists may be part of these movements, but they may be allied with non-Leninist modernizers to whom Leninism should be equally relevant if, indeed, Leninists and non-Leninists can be distinguished at all.[105]

Leninism remained more or less relevant also for modernizing movements that came to power but have not achieved their objectives. This is true where these movements took the form of Communist parties before or after their revolutions, as in Mongolia, Vietnam, Albania, and Cuba.[106] It is also true where they did not call themselves Communist but proclaimed their adherence to Marxism-Leninism, as in Southern

Yemen and Ethiopia, Benin and the Congo, Angola and Mozambique. In many such cases, the regimes' professions of Marxism-Leninism were primarily verbal, its symbols being appealing, especially to the ruling intelligentsia, or they were linked to dependence on economic and military aid from the Soviet Union and Eastern Europe. These professions could fairly easily be dropped when changed foreign-policy needs required it.[107]

The Ethiopian Marxist-Leninist regime, on the other hand, unlike the others and like the Bolsheviks, came to rule not a former colony but a former native empire. It imitated Leninist practice to the extent of collectivizing agriculture, which involved the compulsory resettlement of hundreds of thousands of peasants, and nationalizing what little industry there was. In May 1991, President Mengistu was overthrown, but the new rulers had themselves earlier proclaimed their "Marxism-Leninism."[108]

Leninism and Communism have become separable and often separated, then, the former being an ideology of modernizing intellectuals while Communist parties can come to represent a variety of interests in different societies.[109] (I will deal with Communism in Western Europe in chapter 4.) There are now Communists who are not Leninists, though most of them still use that label to describe themselves, and there are Leninists who are not Communists. Lenin himself, in whose thinking the Party was central, could hardly have imagined its divorce from his ideology, but as one of the early ideologists of the modernizing movement in underdeveloped countries, he laid the foundation for this development.

Chapter Four

Marxism in the East, "Leninism" in the West

MARXISM IN UNDERDEVELOPED COUNTRIES

Adaptable Leninists, Doctrinaire Marxists

So far, I have analyzed Marxism as a product of industrialized societies with a background of aristocratic rule and Leninism as a product of underdeveloped countries under the impact of modernization from without. An obvious objection to my argument would seem to be that there have been adherents of Marxism in underdeveloped countries and people who have thought of themselves as Leninists in industrialized ones.

We need not explain why there may be a few such intellectuals, for individual intellectuals might for any number of reasons be influenced by ideologies that are quite irrelevant to the environments in which they live. The question here is whether Marxism and Leninism have had numerous adherents and played a significant role in the politics of countries where, according to my argument, they should have little or no appeal.

To explain the presence of Marxists in underdeveloped countries, we might first recall that modernizing intellectuals in such countries are always influenced by some variety, Marxist or not, of Western democratic ideology. It is to destroy the antidemocratic elements of traditionalism and colonialism that they hope to, and often do, make their revolutions; in some vague way, they associate democratization with modernization.

Many modernizing intellectuals, often those in the military, expect to bring modernity and democracy to the masses of peasants and workers from above. They may be Leninists and are, in any case, like Leninists in that they both feel that they represent the masses and distrust them. Other modernizers, however, expect the active participation of these masses in their revolutionary endeavors. It is only when they confront not merely the active resistance of their traditional and colonial antagonists but also, more surprising to them, the passive resistance or indifference to their schemes of rapid modernization of great masses of people that some of these modernizers adapt their Western thinking to the reality of underdevelopment.

Such modernizers are then no less convinced than before that, in working for and making their political and social revolutions, they represent the interests of workers and peasants. They now feel, however, that they must act on behalf of these masses, to lead them where they would not go without the intellectuals' leadership, that they may even have to force the masses to act in what the intellectuals see as their true interest. If they employ the Marxian vocabulary, such modernizers become Leninists.

But not all modernizing intellectuals who had faith in the masses undergo this kind of transformation. Some, having been powerfully exposed to Western democratic thought and values, refuse to abandon these and to recognize their irrelevance in their underdeveloped environment. One can speculate that some such persistent Western ideologues are to be found in all modernizing movements. Most of them, being politically ineffective, fall by the wayside before the movement comes to power and never gain much prominence. Some may share in the victory of the revolution but are soon eliminated by the more adaptable victors, as was true of Manuel Urrutia and José Miró Cardona, who found themselves in exile along with the erstwhile enemies of the Cuban Revolution. Some, like Kofi Busia in Ghana and Sutan Sjahrir in Indonesia, may even come to head postrevolutionary governments for some time. But all of them fail to turn their countries into Western democracies. They fail because it is impossible to realize, in their premodern environment, goals and ideals that had gradually grown out of a very different modern environment in the West.

The history of Marxism in underdeveloped countries is but part of this more general history of modern Western ideas in non-Western countries. Before World War I, Marxism remained, to all intents and purposes, unknown in the underdeveloped world, except in the then mostly underdeveloped parts of Europe, that is, in the Balkans and, above all, in Russia, to which I will turn in a moment. After World War I and especially after World War II, Marxism had become an ideology of labor movements well integrated in their advanced industrialized countries. As such, it had little or no appeal in underdeveloped countries. Then it was only Marxian terminology as employed by Leninism that reached and appealed to modernizing intellectuals.

Jawaharlal Nehru, particularly the Nehru of pre-independence India, was one of the few prominent political leaders in an underdeveloped country who was influenced by Marxism rather than Leninism. Still, even Nehru did not turn the Indian National Congress into a social-democratic movement or spread Marxist ideology in India. In Indonesia, Sutan Sjahrir, strongly influenced by Dutch democratic Marxism, lost his power to Leninist Communists and eventually to the non-Leninist modernizer Sukarno. Marxism, with its focus on the advancement of labor and its mass base in labor movements, could not be widely accepted in countries where there were no or very few industrial workers and where it was not class conflict between labor and capital that divided society but the revolt of modernizing forces against still powerful traditionalism and colonialism.

The Mensheviks

Turn-of-the-century Russia was close enough to Western Europe and had enough industrial capitalism and industrial labor to make Marxist thought seem relevant to some of its revolutionary intelligentsia. Thus, in the country where and at the time when Lenin converted the Marxism he received from Marx and German Social Democrats into an ideology of modernizers in underdeveloped countries, there were also intellectually and politically significant Russians who kept the Marxism they received from the West substantially intact.

G. V. Plekhanov was first and foremost among these Russian Marxists, and his outlook, as it concerns us, was generally typical of the Menshevik wing of Russian Social Democracy. He was convinced that Russia, backward as it still was, was by the late nineteenth century firmly on the path of development of Western capitalism and that Marx's analysis and predictions, derived from Western history, applied to Russia. The coming revolution in Russia could only be a bourgeois-democratic one, like the French Revolution. It was to be followed by a period of the rapid growth of capitalism and of the proletariat and a socialist labor movement, which would eventually come to power in a second, socialist revolution. When, like Lenin, Plekhanov used the term "bourgeois democracy," he meant, unlike Lenin, bourgeois democracy. It would be the result of the necessarily impending bourgeois revolution carried out with strong working-class support, not of a peasant revolution resulting in Lenin's revolutionary dictatorship of the proletariat and the peasantry.

Plekhanov recognized that, as in Germany, the bourgeoisie in Russia was not eager to make a revolution against the existing autocratic regime and thought that the working class would have to play a major role in the overthrow of that regime. The immediate task of Russian socialists was to help workers become an independent class-conscious force ready to play that role and to support bourgeois democracy. In the 1905 Revolution, Plekhanov feared that revolutionary workers, possibly seeking to bypass the bourgeois revolution on the road to socialism, had gone beyond what economic conditions permitted and might have unnecessarily frightened the bourgeoisie. As for the peasantry, he saw it mostly as backward and reactionary and as a basis of tsarist autocracy; in the 1905 Revolution, he discounted its potential as an ally of the proletariat.

Above all, Plekhanov, an economic determinist, stressed the limits imposed on political change by social-economic backwardness. This had been a major theme in Marx's thought, but Lenin, as an ideologist of intellectuals dedicated to bringing about massive changes in backward countries, could not abide by it. When Plekhanov argued that Russia was not ripe for socialism, he was obviously right, for he defined socialism, as did Marx and the Marxists, as involving majority rule by an industrial working class. To Lenin and his successors in underdeveloped countries, he was wrong, for to them socialism meant rule by revolutionary modernizing intellectuals, for which Russia was ripe.

Plekhanov and the Mensheviks argued, then, that the socialist revolution could be made only by a strong labor movement, which could grow only in a capitalist and democratic environment that, in turn, could only be the result of a bourgeois-democratic revolution. Lenin counted on his party of intellectuals, supported by the revolutionary "masses," that is, mostly peasants, to come to power in what turned out to be a single revolution and then to industrialize backward Russia. The Mensheviks, on the other hand, required two revolutions to bring about socialism, one bourgeois and one proletarian, with an intervening period of capitalism that would produce industrialization. Clearly, they were faithful disciples of Marx.

Being good Marxists, however, the Mensheviks were poor politicians, for, like Marx and unlike Lenin, they relied on a bourgeoisie and a working class, which were weak in Russia, and, like Marx and unlike Lenin, largely ignored the peasantry[110] and intellectuals, who had strong revolutionary potential in Russia. They assumed that the West European pattern of history, as Marx had distilled it mostly from a combination of British and French experience, would necessarily, mutatis mutandis, be repeated in Russia and, presumably, eventually in even more backward countries.

By now it has become evident that this pattern of a bourgeoisie that had become independent of the old aristocracy, realizing capitalist industrialization and thereby creating a strong labor movement, has, in a world historical perspective, been quite exceptional and that the underdeveloped countries, beginning with Russia, have been moving on a different track of historical change.[111] At the turn of the century, this could not be known, neither by Marxists, in the West or in Russia, nor by Lenin. Neither Lenin nor the Mensheviks clearly perceived that Marx's analysis of history did not apply to underdeveloped Russia; both were caught up in Marxian terminology. Indeed, it was precisely because Bolsheviks and Mensheviks professed adherence to the same ideology that each could explain the others' different policies only as acts of treason.[112]

Still, when it came to a choice between adherence to the Marxian analysis and an effective response to political reality, the Mensheviks tended to choose the former and Lenin the latter. Not surprisingly, the politicians who responded to the reality of underdevelopment, no matter how inappropriate their Western vocabulary may have been—Lenin and the Bolsheviks, like Castro, Sukarno, and Nhkrumah—came to power, while those who not only spoke but thought and tried to act like Western politicians—Plekhanov and the Mensheviks, like Urrutia and Miró, Sjahrir and Busia—failed.

There is no question that there have been Marxists in underdeveloped countries, certainly in Russia until Lenin and his followers eliminated them. Their appearance in such countries does not invalidate my argument that Marxism is a response of workers and intellectuals to the development of industrial capitalism in countries with a history of aristocratic rule in Central and Western Europe. It merely demonstrates that Marxists in underdeveloped countries, under the influence of Marx and of Western, especially German, Social Democrats, responded to this Western European capitalist environment rather than to their own underdeveloped one.

"LENINISM" IN WESTERN EUROPE

Lenin's Marxist Words as Myths

How can one account for the appearance of Leninists in industrial Western Europe if Leninism is a product of underdevelopment? I shall not argue that those who thought of themselves as Leninists were responding to the Russian environment rather than their own Western one, for Lenin, using the vocabulary of Marx, could not convey the underdeveloped reality of Russia to them. On the contrary, that vocabulary concealed this reality and misled some Western socialists to believe that Lenin, like them, was fighting the proletarian class struggle against capital and had led a proletarian revolution to success.

The role, self-conception, and possibly the very existence of Communist parties in industrial Europe illustrate the powerful influence words can have in politics that I noted in chapter 1. To show that words alone, regardless of policies, can have major consequences, let us for a moment suppose that the revolutionaries who seized power in Russia in November 1917 subsequently pursued substantially the same policies that were in fact pursued under Lenin and Stalin, but that they had never heard of Karl Marx and used not his language but that of liberal Western democracy.

Imagine that these revolutionaries called their party "Democratic" or perhaps "Nationalist," but not "Socialist" or "Communist." They claimed to represent the "people," not the "workers." When they repressed all opposition and erected a highly centralized single-party regime, they called it "democracy," not a "dictatorship of the proletariat." When they seized foreign-owned and domestic-owned industry, they did it in the name of "democratization" and "industrialization," not to fight "imperialism" or "capitalism." When they imposed their control on agriculture, they called it "land reform," not "collectivization."

In short, these imaginary revolutionaries in Russia both acted and spoke as many real modernizing revolutionaries have done in other underdeveloped countries. Above all, they never once suggested, as Lenin constantly did, that theirs was a revolution relevant to industrialized countries, that they were the leaders of an international revolutionary working-class movement aiming at the overthrow of capitalism and of the established political order in the West.

Is it not quite probable that the Russian revolutionary regime we have imagined would have aroused little more fear and hostility among conservative propertied and other groups in the West than the regime of Sun Yat-sen, Kemal, or Cárdenas? There were many reasons for the four decades of the Cold War, but the mutual fear and hostility, distrust and dislike that underlay it, beginning with the Russian Revolution, were strongly conditioned by the myths created by Lenin's use of Marxian terminology and accepted, partly in self-fulfilling fashion, both by Lenin and his followers and by their opponents.[113]

A revolutionary regime in Russia pursuing Lenin's policies but not employing Marx's terminology not only would have failed to produce the anti-Communism of the past three quarters of a century but also would have failed to produce Communism. The same Marxist words that aroused the fear and hostility of some attached to the status quo in the West aroused the sympathy and support of some opposed to that status quo. Each side accepted the proletarian-revolutionary myths conveyed by the Marxist words emanating from Russia in part because of the reaction of the other side to them.

Had the November Revolution not been made in the name of an ideology of the Western labor movement, intellectuals and workers in the West who hoped for a proletarian socialist revolution would no more have looked to Lenin as a leader and to his revolution as a model than they looked to Sun Yat-sen, Kemal, or Cárdenas and the Chinese, Turkish, or Mexican revolution. I can argue, then, that the Communist parties in the West perhaps would not have developed when and would certainly not have developed as they did, had Lenin not used the vocabulary of Marx.

Lenin's Non-Leninist Followers

While there were Marxists in underdeveloped countries, there have been no Leninists in Western Europe, though many have applied that term to themselves. Leninism, after all, is not identical with Communism. If Communist parties in underdeveloped countries, like Russia, ceased to be Leninist as their countries became industrialized, Communist parties established in already industrialized countries never were Leninist.

Most of the self-professed Leninists in Western Europe are or were found in the two major West European Communist parties, those of France and Italy (PCF and PCI) and, in the interwar period, in the German Communist Party (KPD). I will deal here only with the PCF and PCI and, in passing, also with the KPD to make the point that these parties are not, and never were, Leninist. This is true also of the Party in Czechoslovakia, the only other industrialized European country with a Communist party of any significant strength that did not result principally from Soviet occupation after World War II. Otherwise, in Europe, Communist parties have at various times been of some political significance only in less industrialized countries: in Iceland and Finland, in Spain and Portugal, in Hungary and Bulgaria, in Greece and Cyprus. Since my concern in this chapter is with the question of Leninism in industrialized countries, I can ignore these Communist parties, though I will very briefly note some similarities between the history of the Spanish Party and that of the PCI and PCF.

European Communist parties typically originated as factions splitting off from existing socialist parties in the immediate post–World War I period. What soon came to define all these early Communist parties was their loyalty to the Soviet Union. It was their common belief in the socialist, proletarian character of the Bolshevik Revolution that held together the new Soviet government and the various Communist parties, all organized in the Third International. The Western Communist parties were, then, in good part founded on what I am here analyzing as the misunderstanding of the identity of Marxism and Leninism or, more generally, of the relevance of the revolutionary politics of Russia, an underdeveloped country, as a model for the politics of labor movements in industrialized countries.

Convinced that they had made a proletarian revolution in Russia, Lenin and the other Bolshevik leaders, especially in the early years after their revolution, relied heavily on hopes of proletarian support in the West and especially in Germany. On the other hand, they felt entitled—indeed, obliged—to give direction to parties in the West intent on making proletarian revolutions of their own. Impressed by their own success, they insisted that these parties adopt the revolutionary methods and approaches that had proved so successful in Russia.

Communist parties gladly subjected themselves to directives emanating from Moscow, for only individuals who believed in the socialist proletarian character of the Russian Revolution and the relevance of Bolshevik methods to their own needs would join a Communist party or would long remain in one. Acceptance of Soviet leadership seemed to them to promise success at home; its rejection was tantamount to isolation from what they saw as a world revolutionary movement that had already triumphed in one-sixth of the globe and was bound to triumph soon in the rest of the world, particularly in Germany with its large labor movement.

There thus arose a situation where political parties in industrialized countries, which in the cases of Germany, France, and Italy at various times had substantial labor support, were directed by and intensely loyal to the leaders of a revolutionary movement in an underdeveloped country. It was a situation hardly conducive to the success of the Western Communist parties. Since this could not be acknowledged or even recognized, however, their failures were typically explained by the "betrayal" or "deviation" of their leaders, who were then purged.

The leaders in Moscow, beginning with Lenin, had all their lives responded to, and finally succeeded in, their underdeveloped environment. They had far less familiarity with Western politics and particularly with the politics of labor movements, which had no relevant equivalent in underdeveloped Russia. But, thinking in terms of Marxian concepts, they regarded themselves as labor leaders and experts in the politics of labor. Because, imbued with their Marxist internationalist notions, they expected the Western proletariat to support revolutionary Soviet Russia against the threats they perceived as emanating from the West, they were deeply interested in Western Communist and labor politics and in the prospects for proletarian revolution in the West, especially in Germany.

Nevertheless, the Bolshevik leaders were inevitably preoccupied with the overwhelming problems at home that confront revolutionaries who come to power expecting and pledged to create in short order a wholly new society with liberty, justice, and prosperity for all, especially for the impoverished masses. As is not unusual in the postrevolutionary period in underdeveloped countries, bitter conflicts divided the leaders of the successful revolutionary party over how to introduce the new society, primarily over alternative policies of industrialization and of controlling agriculture.

The ups and downs of various Bolshevik leaders and factions were reflected in the ups and downs of leaders and factions in the Western Communist parties who were associated with particular Bolshevik leaders and factions. Thus, the repeated splits and purges that beset the German Communist Party in the 1920s and finally culminated in its "Stalinization" were the result primarily of conflicts in underdeveloped Russia over problems arising there and irrelevant to the politics and the labor movement of industrial Germany.

In this peculiar sense, it could be argued, the German Communist Party and also the other Western Communist parties were Leninist, for in some of their behavior they responded to conditions of underdevelopment. It is no doubt also true that some of their leaders shared the Leninist belief that they, as intellectuals, represented the true proletarian class consciousness that the mass of workers could not develop by themselves and that they were therefore called upon to instigate the proletarian revolution, which the proletariat would not make without their leadership.

Nevertheless, if Leninism is seen as an ideology of revolutionary modernizing intellectuals in underdeveloped countries in the early stages of modernization, it is obvious that no party in a country like Germany, not even a Communist party guided from Moscow, for a time by Lenin himself, could be Leninist. The KPD could not advocate the rapid industrialization of already industrialized Germany; it could not seek to develop a mass base among peasants who were not potentially revolutionary; it could not broaden its appeal to all classes, including capitalists, in a struggle with nonexistent colonialist and imperialist enemies.

For my argument here that Communist parties in the West were not and could not be Leninist, it suffices to make these obvious points; it is not necessary to explain at any length the appeal they did have in industrialized countries in spite of the irrelevance of Leninism there. I will touch on the appeal of the PCF and PCI in a moment; in Germany, the KPD attracted elements—intellectuals to its leadership and manual workers, especially unemployed ones, to its mass following—that had been radicalized by their opposition to World War I and then to the parliamentary Weimar Republic, in particular to the nonrevolutionary Social-Democratic Party identified with the latter. They were or became Communists responding to inflation and depression, to right-wing reaction and the rise of Nazism. In the absence of such factors in the post–World War II West German Federal Republic, the KPD virtually disappeared.

The confusion of Leninism with Marxism, the myth of the proletarian character of the Russian Revolution and of the Soviet regime, must surely be a key element in any explanation of the appeal in the West of parties describing themselves as Leninist. It was intellectuals dedicated to the socialist revolution and frustrated by its failure to occur in the West who thought they discovered the road to it in Russia and thus became Communists. And it was workers, long exposed to vague vistas of a socialist revolution that would solve all their problems, who turned to the Russian Revolution as the realization of these vistas and became Communists.

The French and Italian Communist Parties: Heirs of Syndicalism

Like the German Communist Party, the French and Italian ones had their origin in the immediate post–War War I era, but far from disappearing after World War II, like the KPD, the PCF and PCI became major mass parties then, even surpassing their socialist rivals in voting strength, which the KPD never did. Was Leninism, then, more relevant in France and Italy than in Germany?

Seeing Leninism as associated with underdevelopment, I must first note that in the West European context, particularly compared with Britain and Germany, both Italy and France were, indeed, relatively underdeveloped in the interwar and immediate post–World War II period. This means that their agrarian sectors remained quite strong and that much of their industry was relatively small-scale. On the whole, Italy was industrially less developed than France, but it is quite superficial to speak of Italy as one entity in this respect. Much of its North was, even in the 1920s, modern and industrialized, while the South had much in common with what have come to be known as underdeveloped countries. With the exception of these underdeveloped parts of Italy, there was, however, in Italy as well as in France, more industry and more of an organized labor movement than in underdeveloped countries, and, especially in France, much of the peasantry was not landless and impoverished.

To the extent that, in Lenin's lifetime, Italy occupied an intermediate position between the industrial West and the underdeveloped world, Leninism and the Russian Revolution might not have been wholly irrelevant there. In contrast with Germany and the rest of Western Europe, the peasantry was not conservative, and some agricultural laborers may have been potentially revolutionary; and much of the intelligentsia was alienated from society. Still, generally, the early Italian Communists were not Leninists—I will touch on Gramsci in the final section of this chapter—they were not intellectuals who, as Leninists would have done, attempted to mobilize not only workers in the North but also peasants in the South to rebel against their domination by aristocratic landowners and the Church.

In fact, in Italy as well as in France, the Communist Parties grew out of the socialist parties that were close to labor. What they derived from Lenin was not the substance of his ideology but the Marxian language in which he expressed it. They took it for granted that their constituency consisted primarily of workers rather than of peasants, that their enemy was capitalism rather than preindustrial forces. Associated with labor movements from their beginnings, the Communist Parties of France and Italy could not be parties of revolutionary intellectuals leading, with what support, especially among poverty-stricken peasants, they could mobilize, movements for rapid modernization and against native traditional and foreign colonial rulers.

What the relative underdevelopment of France and Italy—and, incidentally, that of Norway—did entail, however, was the fact that, at the time of the Russian Revolution, much of the labor movements of these countries had not fully emerged from the anarcho-syndicalist phase of labor development. That phase, with its small, highly decentralized unions, corresponds to the early small-scale character or uneven development of capitalist industry and typically precedes the social-democratic or Marxist phase of labor development. Because of the more far-reaching industrial development of Britain and Germany, the anarcho-syndicalist phase had been much briefer and weaker in these countries.

Syndicalism can be seen as a reaction of a weak labor movement to its inability to bring about improvements in the status and conditions of labor. Where the trade unions are still small and weak, the early socialist parties lack a substantial constituency. Thus being weak themselves, they are subject to factionalism and splits, which make them even weaker. They are, then, ineffective in serving the labor constituency they would like to represent and fail to attract much support from the relatively few workers and unions there are.

As I noted in chapter 2 with respect to Germany, so in France and Italy the small, new working class that arose by the late nineteenth century suffered from discrimination and exclusion from the institutions of established society. By the beginning of the twentieth century, revolutionary syndicalists responded by rejecting that society and its institutions, including the "state" itself, and by refusing to participate in politics through political parties—even socialist ones—elections, and parliaments. All of these were regarded as instruments of the bourgeoisie; labor could act only through organizations peculiar to it, that is, trade unions, and through trade union methods, especially strikes culminating in a revolutionary general strike.

As in the German Empire, then, early labor in France and Italy reacted to its exclusion from established society by adopting a strongly oppositional attitude often expressed in revolutionary terminology. In Germany, however, with rapidly growing industry and hence a rapidly growing working class, the labor movement expected to benefit from the introduction of parliamentary democracy. It formed a powerful political party, vigorously participated in electoral politics, and demanded the democratization of the Empire. In France and Italy, on the other hand, parliaments and elections—with mostly quite weak socialist parties participating in them—were part of the system the syndicalists rejected.

In the French Third Republic, there was universal manhood suffrage, which was not instituted in Italy until 1919. Universal suffrage, however, held out little promise to workers whose numbers remained small in largely nonindustrial societies with slow economic growth and with strong peasant and petty-bourgeois antilabor majorities. The process of bargaining and compromising in a parliament could not be attractive to a group with little bargaining strength. Thus, while the SPD in Germany stood for democracy, the revolutionary syndicalists in France and Italy saw it as just another bourgeois scheme to be rejected along with all governmental institutions.

Syndicalism, with its antinationalist and antimilitarist commitments, was, especially in France, gravely weakened by World War I, a development to which the influx of unskilled labor into industry may have contributed. Still, deep-seated syndicalist attitudes did not disappear in a few years and came to benefit the new Communist Parties of France and Italy after World War I.

In some respects, these Communist Parties would seem to stand for the very opposite of syndicalism. Syndicalism is but another word for trade unionism, but to Lenin, as quoted above, "trade-unionism means the ideological enslavement of the workers by the bourgeoisie." Why would trade unions that had rejected links to any party and insisted on their autonomy and decentralization now submit to the highly centralized Communist Party? Why would syndicalist or formerly syndicalist workers, who had refused to support socialist or any other parties before the War, now join the Communist Party? Why would they, who had trusted only workers, and certainly not intellectuals, to lead them, now accept intellectual Communist leaders? Had syndicalists not counted on the revolutionary spontaneity of the workers to join a general strike that would put an end to bourgeois society, while Lenin said it was the task of his Party "to combat spontaneity, to divert the working-class movement from this spontaneous trade-unionist striving to come under the wing of the bourgeoisie"?

Still, there were similarities that could make the early Communist parties attractive to revolutionary syndicalists. Lenin's reliance on a small, tightly organized party, mostly of intellectuals, assumes that the "masses" would be ready to respond to its calls to revolutionary action, calls like the ones the early KPD in fact issued a number of times, only to be disappointed by most workers' failure to respond. Like the Communists, the syndicalists, in their small unions, constituted an organized minority that assumed it could lead the unorganized majority of workers. Also, the Leninist emphasis on intellectual minority leadership may have appealed to those under the influence of remnants of Jacobinism and Blanquism in the French socialist tradition.

Other ideological similarities between syndicalists and early Communists involved their antimilitarism and their insistence that class divisions superseded national divisions. The rejection of the state and of "bourgeois" parliamentarism in the early Soviet Union may well have appealed to syndicalists—Lenin's *The State and Revolution* of 1917 contains strong anarcho-syndicalist elements—and the ostensible reliance on soviets, that is, workers' councils, may have appeared to some of them as the realization of their dream of a decentralized society run by trade unions.

What must have attracted alienated workers to revolutionary syndicalism were, however, not so much the finer points of its ideology—which, in any case, were never clearly elaborated—as its total opposition to the existing social, economic, and political system. This total opposition role of syndicalism was, after World War I, assumed by the new Communist Parties. They alone were not tainted by collaboration with the bourgeois enemy, they alone were "revolutionary." It is here that the principal explanation for the French and Italian Communist Parties becoming the successors to syndicalism is to be found.

While the appeal of revolutionary syndicalism to workers alienated from their own societies was largely negative, it also involved hope of a different and better stateless society. That society would be achieved by the workers through the general strike, a prospect, however unrealistic, that served as a powerful myth inspiring workers' confidence and solidarity. After World War I, the Russian Revolution took the place of the general strike. Like the latter, the proletarian character of that revolution and of the new Soviet state was a myth; but, unlike the general strike, the revolution had really taken place and the Soviet state did really exist, which lent great additional inspirational strength to the myth.

The reality of the Russian Revolution as a modernizing revolution in an underdeveloped country, led by intellectuals and not bringing workers to power, and the reality of the Soviet regime as one of modernizers, first revolutionary and then managerial, carrying out rapid industrialization, largely at the expense of workers and peasants, could do little to weaken the myth. Even the leaders of the Revolution, beginning with Lenin, and many of their followers in the Soviet Union were caught up in the myth of their proletarian socialism and therefore reinforced it daily by their words, if not by their deeds. The constant attempts of conservative and other opponents of Western European labor movements to identify these with the Soviet Union also strengthened the myth.

It is not surprising, then, that workers in France and Italy who knew little of what actually happened in faraway Russia and did not really care to know, remained attached to the myth. Intellectuals might lose faith as a reaction to certain events—the crushing of the Kronstadt uprising, the great purges, the Stalin-Hitler pact, the Soviet invasions of Hungary and Czechoslovakia—but workers continued to believe, because they wanted and, given their alienation, needed to believe.

The power of myths, certainly of the one in question here, is a function not so much of their closeness to or distance from reality as of their ability to fill strong psychic and social needs. As long as French and Italian workers felt like deprived and underprivileged aliens in their own countries, they needed the satisfaction of believing that they had a powerful fatherland of their own on the other side of Europe and the hope this implied for a drastic, if ill-defined, future change in their own countries.

Because Communist parties used to follow directives from Moscow, they were commonly seen as tools of the Soviet Union. That view, however, did not explain why they followed these directives so willingly and even eagerly. To explain that, one must understand that the Soviet Union was also a tool of the Communist parties in the sense that its existence served the needs of their members and that the parties' Soviet links were therefore a source of strength to them.

PCF and PCI: From Syndicalism to Disappearance or Social Democracy

The Communist Parties of France and Italy, claiming to represent the policies of the Russian Revolution and the Soviet state in their own countries, became the successors to the syndicalists, as the myth of the proletarian socialist nature of the Russian Revolution and the Soviet state became the successor to the myth of the general strike. To alienated workers, the Communist Parties now served the same function the syndicalists had served, to provide for them a society in which they could feel at home, within and opposed to the hostile larger society.

The PCF and, when it was not suppressed by Fascism, the PCI served that function in the interwar period and the first post–World War II decade on a larger scale and in more highly organized fashion than the syndicalists had ever done before World War I. Unlike the syndicalists, they participated in elections and parliaments and refrained from the use of violence, reflecting the fact that the still alienated workers they represented were already strong enough to compete on more even terms with socialist and "bourgeois" parties and already had made gains not to be risked in violent confrontations. In France, the Communists could also see the Russian Revolution as a continuation or fulfillment of the French Revolution and thus could link themselves to the French revolutionary tradition.

The role of the PCF and the PCI in their first four decades (except under the Vichy and Fascist regimes and Nazi German occupation) was, then, somewhat similar to that of the Social Democrats in imperial Germany.[114] Like the SPD, the two Communist Parties provided a counterculture and a countersociety for their constituency, alienated from the dominant culture and society, yet they participated in the existing political system. Just as the Marxian vocabulary of class struggle and revolution was, as I stressed in chapter 2, attractive to the SPD's constituents then, so it was now to the PCF's and PCI's constituents.

That these two Communist Parties became the effective representatives of the more alienated sections of the French and Italian working classes was not due to Leninism as an ideology of revolutionary intellectuals in underdeveloped countries. It was, rather, due to the fact that this ideology was expressed by Lenin in the Marxian terminology quite inappropriate to his situation and his policies. That, in turn, permitted representatives of industrial workers, for whom the laborite terminology of Marx was quite appropriate, to identify themselves with Lenin and his revolution.

Like the SPD before World War I, the PCF and PCI thus benefited from the appeal of Marxian conceptions but, unlike the SPD, they could also associate themselves with a successful revolution. Because this revolution was such a powerful myth, it did not matter that it was, in fact, irrelevant as a model in France and Italy and that, like the SPD in imperial Germany, the PCF and PCI did not know how to make the revolution they kept talking about.

Both their association with Marxism through the Marxian terminology and with the Soviet Union were sources of strength for the PCF and PCI as long as much of French and Italian labor was alienated. Beginning in the 1950s, France and Italy underwent rapid industrialization. The industrial working class gained in numerical and organizational strength, and the antilabor peasantry and petty bourgeoisie shrank, their members joining the working class or the white-collar middle class, which are not clearly distinct and share many interests. Workers, no longer weak and isolated but materially better off, better represented in government, and more and more integrated into the larger society, had less and less reason to feel alienated.

This new situation confronted the PCF and PCI with a choice. They could continue their association with Marxist terminology and with the Soviet Union, though more and more workers, now feeling at home in their own country, no longer needed that distant mythical workers' fatherland. The Parties could thus remain the home of a now shrinking alienated constituency and retain what they could regard as their ideological purity at the cost of growing weakness. Or they could change as their laborite constituency changed; they could, like the SPD in the Weimar Republic, engage in coalition politics and, like the SPD in the present Federal Republic, turn from a workers' party into a "people's party."

The Italian Communists have followed the latter course with remarkable consistency, to the point where they explicitly renounced their association with Lenin and the Soviet Union. In early 1991, they replaced the hammer and sickle with an oak tree that is far more Green than Red, and even gave up the "Communist" label for that of the Democratic Party of the Left (PDS). While it was to become a new, broader political formation of the Left, a more orthodox faction split off to form Rifondazione comunista.

In the 1960s and especially the 1970s, the French Communists moved in the same direction, then called "Eurocommunist," but subsequently reversed their course and took the alternative route of retreat into a shrinking proletarian ghetto. As a result, especially now that their workers' fatherland in the East has disappeared, they seem well on the way to changing from a mass party into an outdated sect, a trend likely to be accompanied by internal divisions and conflict.

Italy and France having become fully industrialized, their labor movements have passed from the syndicalist into the social-democratic phase of labor development, although minorities within them may still be attached to syndicalist notions of extraparliamentary action. The first half-century of the Italian and French Communist Parties proved to be a transitional period between these two phases. The PCI has been sufficiently flexible to become a "people's party" and, in the future, in one form or another and under whatever name, the party of Italian social democracy or a major element of it. The PCF has been unable to adapt, and it is the French Socialist Party that has, at the PCF's expense, come to represent the social-democratic segment of the electorate, which, as in Germany and Italy, extends well beyond the shrinking labor movement.

This is not the place to try to explain why the PCF and the PCI have pursued such different policies with such different results in recent years. I suspect that the PCI's longer experience with Fascism; its role in writing Italy's more durable post-Resistance constitution; its deeply entrenched position, crossing class lines, in the society and in the local governments of central Italy; the existence of a left, laborite wing among its clerical opponents; and the relative weakness of the Italian Socialists have attracted the Italian Communists far more than the French ones to attempts to broaden their appeals and to enter coalitions with other parties.

However that may be, it is obvious that both in Italy and in France, now that they are advanced industrialized countries, Leninism is irrelevant. My point here was to show that it had been irrelevant to the PCF and the PCI all along, even when they thought of themselves as Leninist but were in fact first the heirs of syndicalism and then played a role akin to that of the Social Democrats in the German Empire. They were, after all, genuine workers' parties, while Leninism is an ideology of intellectuals who may think of themselves as representing workers and hence employ the language of Marxism, but function in an environment where workers hardly exist.

If the Russian Communists wrongly believed they were Marxists when they were really modernizing Leninists, the French and Italian Communists believed they were Leninists when they were really laborite Marxists, at least when and to the extent that they favored not only labor but also parliamentary democracy. If Marxian terminology could appeal to Leninists who thought it turned them into Marxists, it is not surprising that, coming to them via Lenin, it could also appeal to Marxists who thought it turned them into Leninists. To be sure, the more they—especially in the PCI—came to believe in parliamentary democracy, the less they thought of themselves as Leninists.

Parenthetically, I may here briefly note that there are certain parallels between the history of the PCF and especially that of the PCI, on the one hand, and, on the other, that of the Spanish Communist Party (PCE), a party we can otherwise ignore here, for it never achieved much popular strength. Though Spain could once be regarded as an underdeveloped country with powerful traditional forces, and Leninism was hence to an extent relevant there, the Spanish Communist Party, like its two larger sister parties, never was a party of revolutionary intellectuals seeking to mobilize a mass modernizing movement with peasant and bourgeois support.

In the 1920s, when the PCE was established, much of Spain, like much of Italy, was industrially underdeveloped. Like the PCI, the PCE, however, did not take a Leninist course but attached itself to the labor movement. There being even less industry in Spain than in Italy (though it, too, was regionally concentrated), the working class was small and syndicalism was strong in it, as was anarchism in some of the rural population.

Unlike the PCF and PCI, the PCE could never take the place of syndicalism, but could only exist side by side with it as a weak competitor. In the Spanish Civil War, it was greatly strengthened, much as the PCF and PCI were during the World War II Resistance. But these two Parties emerged victorious and powerful from this period into one of parliamentary democracy. They were soon larger than their socialist rivals and well established as their countries underwent rapid industrialization. The Spanish Civil War, on the other hand, was followed by nearly four decades of Franco's dictatorship, from which the PCE emerged with about one-third the voting strength of the Socialists.

Like the PCI, the PCE has responded to the rapid industrialization of its country by pursuing "Eurocommunist" and coalitional policies. Unlike the PCI, however, being weak, it has as a result suffered from splits and internal conflicts. The discrediting of the Soviet Communist Party and the failure of its coup attempt in 1991 contributed to the weakness and division of the PCE—and, indeed, of the PCF. Not only did Communist parties in Western Europe remain identified with the Soviet Union in the minds of some people who might otherwise have joined them or voted for them, but some of their leaders continued to link themselves to certain factions or tendencies within Soviet Communism and then suffered from their defeats.

It is probably still a little too early, but it seems not unreasonable to predict the Communism in France and Italy may be disappearing—in France because the Party may be shrinking to political insignificance, in Italy because it may be dissolving into a larger, less well-defined entity. A hundred years after syndicalism became an influential factor in the French and Italian labor movements, the conditions that gave rise to it have disappeared, and with them their result—an alienated segment of the working class.

That segment was long the core of the PCF's and the PCI's mass constituency (though my exclusive emphasis on it here is, no doubt, an oversimplification) and, while that was the case, the Parties had to retain their Marxist vocabulary and their attachment to the Soviet Union. As that core has declined and disappeared, and its members in the Party have either been replaced by nonalienated workers and, more and more, by nonworkers, as has happened in Italy, or have not been replaced at all, as has been true in France, the Parties have become doomed to disappear.

Since World War II the PCF and the PCI have been the only Communist parties of major significance in Western Europe. If they do disappear as such (and as the Communist parties of East Germany, Poland, the Czech Republic, Hungary, and perhaps Croatia and Slovenia disappear or change their character), Communist parties with any popular strength under whatever name will remain only in some underdeveloped countries and, in Europe, in some that were underdeveloped when the Communists came to power there: the former Soviet republics, Romania, Bulgaria, Slovakia, and what is left of Yugoslavia, particularly Serbia.

The PCF, the PCI, and also the Czech Communist Party—and, until the 1930s, the KPD—were the only Communist parties that were genuine labor parties, not merely parties that professed to represent the working class. With their disappearance, the link between Communism and labor is broken. There never was a necessary link between Leninism and labor; only the verbal link between them may remain. Only in nonindustrial countries, where there are few or no workers, may Communist and non-Communist Leninists claim to represent the mostly nonexistent working class. Since, on the other hand, the historic link of labor to Marxism and its social-democratic successor movements in the West is beyond doubt, it is becoming clearer and clearer that the link between Marxism and Leninism is merely a verbal one, that substantively they are quite different ideologies representing quite different interests in different environments.

BETWEEN MARXISM AND LENINISM

I have now dealt with industrialized and underdeveloped countries and argued that Marxism is an ideology appropriate to the former and Leninism is appropriate to the latter. But what about countries that are still more or less underdeveloped, yet already to some degree industrialized? Is there an ideology intermediate between Marxism and Leninism, sharing some characteristics of each, that is appropriate to such countries? Do intellectuals in them respond to their underdevelopment, like Leninists, in the fashion I described in chapter 3 and yet simultaneously respond to the existence of a native bourgeoisie and especially a native labor movement as Marxists did in Europe and as I indicated in chapter 2?

Unlike the modernizing intellectuals in underdeveloped countries who have often called themselves "Marxists-Leninists," though they are simply Leninists, such intermediate figures would be the only ones who truly deserve to be described as "Marxists-Leninists." While my object here is to distinguish between Marxism and Leninism, the possibility of elements of both of these ideologies being combined needs to be at least briefly explored to see if the gap between them can be bridged. A quick look at the ideologies of the Chilean Left and of Antonio Gramsci may throw some light on the problem.

Chile could be described as a country sharing features of capitalist industrialism with Western Europe and of a colonial-agrarian order with some of the industrially more backward countries of Latin America. By the mid-twentieth century, Chile had almost as large a percentage of its labor force in manufacturing as Italy, and hardly a larger percentage engaged in agriculture than France and a much smaller one than Italy. Its industry was based on powerful native capitalism, and about a third of its industrial labor force and a fifth of its total work force was organized in trade unions. On the other hand, a major segment of its economy was "colonial," for the copper and nitrate mining industries were owned first by British and then by American firms. Agricultural landownership was highly concentrated, as is often true in underdeveloped countries under traditional rule, but there was considerable overlap between the industrial and the landed oligarchies.[115]

Corresponding to this ambiguous situation, what was commonly described as the "Marxist" Left in Chile, made up of the Communist and Socialist parties, can be said to have been half Marxist and half Leninist— or "Marxist-Leninist"—in its programs and policies. The two parties were the main components of the Popular Unity coalition government headed by Salvador Allende from 1970 to 1973. Like Marxists, in opposition to the native bourgeoisie, that government was pledged to and did raise the standard of living of the working class through social welfare measures and the encouragement of trade unionization, and it favored and carried out the nationalization of banks, public utilities, and monopolies. Like Leninists, it sought to and did nationalize the foreign-owned extractive industries and to expropriate and divide the large landed estates. The Allende coalition, in sum, adopted the pro-labor policies of Marxism and the anticolonial and antitraditional policies of Leninism.[116]

Italy in the 1920s was also partly underdeveloped and partly industrialized. Lenin's Italian contemporary and admirer, Antonio Gramsci, a native of underdeveloped Sardinia active in industrial Turin, was a "Marxist-Leninist," though perhaps more of a Leninist than a Marxist. Indeed, with regard to the Leninist reliance on the power of the will, Gramsci was far more explicit, more Leninist, than Lenin. Much more openly than Lenin could have done, the young Gramsci, not yet tied to a party line, writing immediately after the Bolshevik seizure of power, could hail the October Revolution as "the revolution against Karl Marx's *Capital*" and could proclaim that "will becomes the motor of the economy, the shaper of objective reality, which lives and moves and acquires the character of volcanic matter in eruption that can be channeled where the will likes and as the will likes."[117]

Also like Lenin, Gramsci emphasized the importance of a disciplined vanguard party led by intellectuals,[118] but he was evidently more concerned with mass participation in the party, and his intellectuals were not only, like Lenin's, an outside force acting on the proletariat but also the proletariat's own "organic" intellectuals linked with the masses.

Gramsci's masses are, much more like Marx's and unlike Lenin's, industrial workers. Like Lenin, he hopes that workers can lead the peasants into a revolutionary alliance, but his principal concern is with the workers of industrial northern Italy, not with the peasants of the underdeveloped South. The workers are to express and act on their solidarity in factory councils, the organizational base both of the revolution and of the future society. Here Gramsci is closer to the syndicalist tradition than to Lenin's reliance on the Party or to the Marxist emphasis on parliamentary democracy, which he, like both Lenin and the syndicalists, rejects.

On the other hand, Gramsci's conception of cultural and intellectual "hegemony" to be attained by the future proletarian ruling class in a "war of position" to overcome bourgeois hegemony seems to imply a gradualist conception of the revolution much more akin to the Marxist tradition of labor movements in industrialized countries than the Leninist one of revolutionary intellectuals in underdeveloped countries. Undeniably, both Leninist and Marxist—and also syndicalist—elements are intermingled in Gramsci's thought.

The central difference between Marxism and Leninism is the political one, that is, the difference between the interests represented by them. On this key point, Gramsci remains inconsistent. He favors as the agent of revolution and as the central institution of the future society both the Leninist intellectual-led disciplined vanguard party and the factory councils that would represent organized as well as unorganized workers regardless of their party affiliation.

These incompatible positions can perhaps be reconciled verbally, but in practice they are irreconcilable, a problem Gramsci himself did not have to confront. Lenin, once in power in underdeveloped Russia, quickly abandoned the workers' soviets (councils) and erected a Party dictatorship that subsequently advanced industrialization in good part at workers' expense. Gramsci's Italian Communist Party, on the other hand, adapting to Italy's rapid economic development and parliamentary government after World War II, eventually abandoned the Leninist format of the party (though a syndicalist council-oriented strand remains significant in what was the PCI) and became a laborite social-democratic party in the Marxist tradition. Responding to their different environments, Lenin followed one course and the PCI the other, but Gramsci's combination of laborism and Leninism was not viable in either an underdeveloped or an industrial environment.

An ideology cannot be "Marxist-Leninist," then; it can be Marxist or Leninist but not both. It can represent only workers in industrialized countries or intellectuals in underdeveloped countries, because these groups, facing wholly different problems in different environments, have quite different interests.

Like Gramsci, some intellectuals on the Chilean Left could, no doubt, ignore these differences. They could claim to favor both workers and peasants, though many interests of these two classes are different. They could attack both the bourgeoisie as the workers' antagonist and the landlords as the opponents of the modernizing intelligentsia by lumping the two upper classes together as the "oligarchy" (not a term Marx used), because in Chile they were, in part, composed of the same people. They could stand for nationalization of industry as a general principle, though it serves quite different functions for Marxists and Leninists. In the Marxist tradition, which does not contemplate foreign-owned, colonial industry, the socialization—not necessarily in the form of nationalization—of domestic industry is designed to empower workers. To Leninists, nationalization of foreign-owned industry is meant to provide independence from colonial ties for a government of modernizing intellectuals, and nationalization of any industry by such a government in an underdeveloped country is to advance its program of industrialization, not to improve the status of labor.

Because Marxism and Leninism are so very different, elements of both are usually not adhered to by the same individuals, as they were to some extent by Gramsci. Even in Chile, where a combination of such elements was relatively easy, different individuals and different parties evidently inclined more to Marxism or to Leninism. Any generalization in this regard about the two major parties is bound to oversimplify a complex situation, especially with respect to the Socialist Party, which had a history of splits and factionalism and whose leader, Allende, was closer to the Communists than to many Socialists. It seems by and large true, however, that the Socialist Party, or at least its wing that sympathized with Castro, tended to be more Leninist, while the Communist Party, perhaps somewhat closer to organized labor and forming the more moderate, "reformist," and gradualist wing of the Popular Unity coalition, tended to be more Marxist.

Turn-of-the-century Russia was not as advanced industrially as Italy in Gramsci's day or, certainly, as Chile in Allende's. Still, industrialization was progressing and an industrial proletariat was growing rapidly enough to make the laborite Marxian ideology attractive to some intellectuals. On the other hand, the impact of modernization on underdeveloped Russia produced as a reaction a movement of modernizing intellectuals, of Leninists. Marxists and Leninists soon formed two distinct antagonistic political groupings, the Mensheviks and the Bolsheviks. Initially, however, confronting the common enemy of the tsarist autocracy and anxious to distinguish themselves from other Russian revolutionary movements, Marxists and Leninists were not clearly aware of what separated them from each other. All of them thought of themselves as Marxists and all of them adopted the vocabulary of Karl Marx, mental habits they retained even when they came to fight each other bitterly.

In Russia, Italy, and Chile, in the different time periods I have referred to, there was room for both Marxist and Leninist ideology. Since the adherents of both shared their opposition to the status quo and even thought of themselves as "revolutionary," they could at times overlook or minimize their differences, especially because they used the same terminology. In highly industrialized societies, however, there was room only for Marxism, in underdeveloped countries only Leninism is appropriate, and thus the difference between the two ideologies is very clear. That they employ the same language and that, in the fairly exceptional thought of Gramsci or the Chilean Left, elements of both ideologies precariously coexisted need not confuse us into seeing the two as one. The presence of some industry and some workers in Russia did, however, allow Lenin to think of himself as a Marxist and to build a verbal bridge between Marxism and his own quite different ideology of Leninism.

Chapter Five

Why Marxism and Leninism Have Been Seen as a Single Ideology

IDEOLOGY AND ENVIRONMENT

Ideology: Words or Substance?

My argument that Leninism is not identical with Marxism, or is not one variety or interpretation of it, or even a deviation from it seems fairly obviously supported by their different histories. That they have appealed to different kinds of people confronting different problems has become increasingly clear from their beginnings, respectively in Lenin and in Marx and Engels, down to the present. Having argued this point at great length, I nevertheless cannot reasonably expect it to be widely accepted.

The belief that Marxism and Leninism are a single ideology is too deeply rooted to be easily given up and is widely held among people who consider themselves Leninists or Marxists and by others who see themselves as anti-Leninists and anti-Marxists and, most important to me, by scholars who have studied Marxism and Leninism, not to mention journalists and those who read their writings. To make my argument more persuasive, then, I must attempt to answer the question why a view I have tried to prove wrong or at least inappropriate for purposes of political analysis is so deeply rooted and so widely held.

Whether one sees Marxism and Leninism as one ideology or two distinct ones depends on one's conception of ideology. I could insist that they are two ideologies, only because I define an ideology with reference to the interests and functions it serves in a specific political and social environment. There is, however, a strong tradition in the study of political thought that ignores or minimizes the effects of ideas on their social context. Seen in this light, Marxism and Leninism may appear much more closely related than I see them.

Often the history of political thought is written as the history of ideas developed by individual thinkers, more or less completely ignoring the societies and the conflicts within them, to which the thinkers in question responded, and the social groupings with which they were associated and which their thoughts represented and appealed to. Some treatments of Plato or Aristotle barely mention the Athenian society that must have shaped their thought; Hobbes or Locke is sometimes discussed without any reference to the English Civil War and its consequences. Ideas taken out of their social context can be treated as if they were absolutely valid or eternally relevant. Concepts divorced from their original context can be transferred from one context to another. Aristotle's views of slavery or democracy can, at least implicitly, be seen as if they necessarily applied to slavery or democracy in the United States.

Since students of ideas are quite generally and quite naturally more interested in ideas than in social, political, and economic conditions, they may be inclined to explain ideas in terms of ideas. They think of political ideas as developing out of other political ideas independently of, or merely as a cause of and not as a reaction to, environmental political conditions. They see a thinker not so much as deriving his or her ideas from the surrounding world as from the ideas of other thinkers. Thinkers themselves may attribute their ideas to the influence of other thinkers. Obviously, such an explanation of a particular thinker's ideas may be more or less valid, the effect of the environment and the influence of other ideas on a thinker being a matter of degree and not mutually exclusive.

In this essay, I have not been interested in the ideas of two individuals, Marx and Lenin, as such, nor do I question the obvious fact that Lenin was influenced by Marx. Rather, I am concerned with two ideologies, with how Marx's and Lenin's ideas reflected certain interests in particular types of societies and were adopted by certain people because they served a certain function in these societies. This essay is meant to be a contribution not to a history of political thought that traces ideas from one thinker to another, but to an explanation of the appeal and relevance of ideas to people in certain situations in certain times and places.

In considering an ideology and its relevance and appeal in certain conditions, it is important to distinguish between its words and its substance. For example, the single word "proletariat" stands for a different substance in Marxist and in Leninist ideology. Both the words and the substance of ideas can be passed from one thinker to another if they live in the same kind of environment. Both can also be transmitted to thinkers who ignore their own different environment or misinterpret it in the light of the ideas that influenced them. Those thinkers' ideas are then not likely to be very influential in their own environment, except among a relatively few who are, in turn, willing and able to ignore or misinterpret it.

Thus, when ideas are transplanted from one environment to a very different one, their words and their substance can be retained, but they will then not have broad appeal. Or their words can be retained, but in response to the new environment a new substance can be infused into them; and that new substance, if it is relevant to the environment, can, along with the old words, become a widely appealing ideology.

Earlier, I noted how, when Marxian ideas arrived in Russia, their words and substance were retained by the Mensheviks and their words were retained but their substance was replaced by Lenin. The Mensheviks failed and Lenin succeeded in Russia, and Leninism as an ideology spread through the underdeveloped world, while Marxist Menshevism never found any resonance there. Another example of the substance of words changing, while the words have not, that is even more telling, because it involves changes across millennia rather than a century, is the fate of the Bible. The words of the Old and New Testament have remained unchanged through all this time, but how they have been understood, what has been believed and acted upon, has differed widely from time to time, from place to place, from social group to social group.

Were no new substance ever infused into old words, these words might eventually die as they become irrelevant, but with their new substance they can survive into new times and new environments. Words, then, have a way of lasting longer or spreading farther than the substance they were originally associated with. Perhaps for that reason or perhaps because to some the words may be more interesting than the substance, both observers of and participants in the evolution of ideologies have often focused on the former at the expense of the latter. Certainly words tend to conceal differences in substance, and it is far easier to trace the persistence of words than the often more subtle changes in substance. Furthermore, politicians, generally reluctant to admit to themselves and to others that they have changed their positions, tend to assert their orthodoxy by clothing new ideas or policies in old words.

Those who use the same words, regardless of substance, come, then, to be designated by the same label, particularly if they claim that label for themselves. Thus, St. Augustine and St. Thomas Aquinas, Innocent III and Martin Luther, Orthodox bishops in Russia, Baptist preachers in Alabama, liberation theologians in Latin America, and the Coptic clergy in Ethiopia—they are all "Christians." And all the people I listed at the beginning of this essay, from Marx and Luxemburg through Gramsci and Lenin and Mao to Pol Pot and Mengistu—they are all "Marxists."

Marxism and Leninism are one ideology, if an ideology is defined in terms of its words rather than its substance and if its history is seen as that of its words being passed from one thinker to another, for example, from Marx to Lenin, regardless of the different environments these thinkers responded to. If Lenin is read without regard to the fact that he was the product of late-nineteenth-century Russia, he may well appear as a Marxist—not a profound or consistent Marxist theorist, but a Marxist politician writing about the development of capitalism and the position of the bourgeoisie and the proletariat, about class struggle and revolution.

Analysts may, then, contrary to my view, see Marxism and Leninism as a single ideology for two quite different reasons, one involving a misunderstanding on their part, the other the employment of a definition of ideology different from mine. In the one case, they may simply fail to see the differences between Marxism and Leninism. They may read Marx into Lenin and his followers, which is easily done because Leninists frequently quote Marx in support of their positions. They may also read Lenin and Leninists into Marx, ascribing views of the former to the latter. They are deceived by the common words and ignore the difference in substance, because they do not relate the ideologies to their environments.

Other analysts, however, may regard Marxism and Leninism as one and the same ideology because they define an ideology in terms of its vocabulary. If Lenin and Leninists inherited Marx's terminology, then, by that definition, they inherited his ideology. Such analysts may or may not be aware of differences between Marxism and Leninism, they may put more or less emphasis on the different substance expressed by the common words, on the different social environments to which Marxism and Leninism responded, on the different needs, interests, values, policies, and goals they represented. The more they emphasize these, the closer they come to my view of the relationship of Marxism to Leninism. They might even agree with almost everything I have written here, but prefer to see the differences I have stressed as occurring within a single ideology.

It is not wrong, and may well be useful for certain purposes, to define an ideology by the words it employs. Coptic priests, liberation theologians, and Baptist preachers do have something in common, and, if that is to be emphasized, it makes sense to call them all Christians. But attaching the same label to them will not help explain—indeed, it will tend to conceal—their vastly different political roles in their different societies. In a study of Christian theology, the professed beliefs of various kinds of Christians and the words they use to profess them, rather than their political roles, are central, and their common beliefs may well be used to define the Christian religion. But in a study of political ideologies, it is far more useful to define ideologies by their substance than by their words.

For purposes of political analysis, then, I believe that it is preferable and simply more straightforward and sensible to regard two sets of very different ideas, even if they employ the same words, as two ideologies; to ascribe not one but two ideologies to two very different types of movements functioning, with very different interests and policies, in two very different types of societies. Seeing the two ideologies as one makes it more difficult to explain or even to recognize these differences.

Lenin's role in history as a successful revolutionary in underdeveloped Russia is difficult to understand if we see him as a champion of industrial workers in a class struggle with capitalism, even if he did see himself in this light. Karl Marx, writing in nineteenth-century England about contemporary and future industrial capitalism, will be misunderstood if he is seen as an analyst of anticolonial and antitraditional modernizing revolutions in underdeveloped countries or as an advocate of the kind of single-party system that has typically emerged out of such revolutions.

Surely those who would understand the policies of self-professed Marxist regimes in China and Cuba, in Afghanistan and Ethiopia, will gain as little insight by reading Marx or Engels as those who look for an explanation of the history of German Social Democracy in the writings of Mao Zedong or the speeches of Fidel Castro. Only those who confuse Leninism and Marxism and their very different concepts of revolution could think, as some writers do, that it was puzzling or paradoxical that Leninist revolutions could occur in underdeveloped countries when Marx had expected revolutions in advanced industrial ones.

Marxists' Un-Marxian View of Marxism and Leninism

No widely appealing ideology, as distinguished from an individual thinker's work, can be explained without reference to its social context, but it is particularly ironic that Marxism has often been dealt with in this fashion. After all, one of Marx's central ideas and one of his most fruitfully suggestive ones is his view of ideology as superstructural, that is, as explicable with reference to a social and economic base. Marx's theory and the sociology of knowledge that he influenced see ideologies not as arbitrary products of the human mind but as responses to the social environment in which they are produced and received.

Anyone touched by the approaches of Marxism and/or of the sociology of knowledge ought at least to view with some suspicion claims that leaders and ideologists of very different movements in different types of societies adhere to the same ideology, that a single ideology was widely accepted by great numbers of people occupying very different positions in countries at very different levels of economic development.

That labor movements in industrialized countries and modernizing movements in underdeveloped countries, representing quite different interests and pursuing quite different goals, could be inspired by the same ideology, seems, on its face, improbable. Such a coincidence would surely call for an explanation, especially by Marxists, as it is incompatible with Marx's conception of history and of ideology. Yet Marxists and non-Marxists alike have generally accepted it without question as a fact, simply because the ideologists of some labor movements and those of some modernizing movements employ a similar vocabulary. Thus, many a book on Marxism contains chapters on Lenin, and many a book on Leninism or even on Soviet politics begins with a chapter on Karl Marx's thought.

Even authors who regard themselves as Marxists of one variety or another often discuss and contrast the ideas of thinkers, like Kautsky and Lenin, without so much as noting the very different environments in which such thinkers functioned.[119] They treat their ideas not as relative to their environments but as absolutely true or false. If Lenin and Kautsky disagreed—for instance, if Lenin said that the dictatorship of the proletariat was rule by the Communist party and Kautsky said it was parliamentary democracy—one must, in that view, be right and the other one wrong. Such thinkers are then seen as if they were not ideologists but natural scientists who, starting out from an agreed-upon body of knowledge and assumptions, seek to extend the range of their science in ways that other scientists, in the light of accepted theory and evidence, may or may not regard as valid.

A book on the history of ''Marxism''—and there are many such books—with chapters on Marx and Engels, Kautsky, Lenin, Mao, and probably other Marxist and Leninist thinkers is not like a book on the history of physics with chapters on, say, Newton, Faraday, Bohr, Einstein, Planck, and others. The latter deals with the contributions of different individuals to the understanding of a single set of phenomena employing a single terminology with agreed-upon meaning. That these individuals lived in different times and different countries is irrelevant to an appreciation of their contributions, though it may well have affected their ability to make these contributions.

A book on the history of ''Marxism,'' on the other hand, deals with the thought of different individuals on different phenomena designated by the same words. That these thinkers lived in and responded to different environments is hence vitally important for an understanding of their thought, which cannot, like propositions about the physical universe, be said to be absolutely valid or invalid.

All too often the authors and the readers of books on the history of ''Marxism,'' of ''Marxism-Leninism,'' or of Communism may think of them as if they were books on the history of natural science, as if they dealt with the evolution of a single ideology (or even a single science). To my way of thinking, this is confusing, but it is particularly inexcusable in the case of writers and readers who regard themselves as Marxists. They should not analyze what they should view as the superstructural element of ideology without reference to the socioeconomic base that, according to Marx, accounts for it.

THE USES AND ORIGINS OF THE CONFUSION

Why Leninists in Underdeveloped Countries and Some Western Marxists Want To Be "Marxists-Leninists"

Why would politicians and ideologists facing quite different problems in quite different environments want to think, speak, and write employing the same concepts and words? Why would they want to use words with an original meaning quite clearly irrelevant to them, like the words "proletariat" and "workers" in a society without workers? Why would they want to see themselves and to be seen as adherents of the same ideology? I shall try to answer this question in the next section specifically with reference to the time when Leninism and its differences from Marxism first appeared, by showing why it was difficult for those on each side, even when they were in conflict, not to think of themselves and of each other as Marxists. Here, I want to deal with the question more generally and, to do so, merely need to recall some points made above.

Why would Leninists want to think of themselves as Marxists? Western-oriented and, in this sense, modernizing intellectuals in underdeveloped countries typically attach themselves more or less consistently to some Western ideology, and nineteenth-century Russian intellectuals, being geographically and culturally relatively close to Western Europe, did so in great numbers. Every Western European ideology, from anarchism through socialism and liberalism to conservatism, had adherents in Russia. As, by the turn of the century, there were some capitalist industry and the beginnings of a labor movement in Russia, it is not surprising that some Russian intellectuals adopted Marxism as their ideology and the newly powerful German Social-Democratic Party as their model.

Once Lenin was in power, and especially when he was succeeded by Stalin, their revolution became the first major successful modernizing revolution in an underdeveloped country. The policies and institutions associated with the industrialization of the Soviet Union—the centralized single party, the five-year plans, collectivization of agriculture, anti-Westernism—were all clothed in the Marxian vocabulary that had arrived in Russia in the late nineteenth century. Just as Leninism became the official ideology, the language of Marxism became the official and sole language of the Soviet regime. The Marxist-Leninist vocabulary long survived the replacement of the Leninist revolutionary substance by a technocratic-managerial one, for words often survive, and thereby help conceal, changes in substance.

As Soviet policies and institutions were relevant and attractive to revolutionary intellectuals in underdeveloped countries, the latter also accepted the language in which they were clothed. That Marxist language, too, was attractive to them, all the more so as it had been adapted by Lenin to the reality of underdevelopment. Revolutionary modernizing intellectuals in underdeveloped countries, then, wanted to be Leninists, not Marxists. Most of them, no doubt, knew little of Marxism or of Marx, who had little to say that was of interest to them. But as Lenin thought he was a Marxist and used the language of Marx, the intellectuals who wanted to be followers of Lenin also thought of themselves as Marxists or as "Marxists-Leninists" and used Marxist language.

Marxism and Leninism are merged into a single ideology not only in the minds of Leninists in underdeveloped countries who think of themselves, and talk like, Marxists but also in the minds of would-be Marxists who think of themselves, and talk like, Leninists—and, in fact, are not Leninists and may not be Marxists either. This, too, I have already touched on.

There is not only a historical pattern of alienated modernizing intellectuals in underdeveloped countries looking to the West for models for their salvation; there is also one of alienated socialist intellectuals in the West looking to underdeveloped countries for the realization of their hopes and dreams. Frustrated because the socialism they had expected had not come to their own countries, they have, since 1917, successively turned to and then been disillusioned by Lenin's and even Stalin's Russia, Cárdenas' Mexico, Mao's China, Castro's Cuba, Ho's North Vietnam, Nyerere's Tanzania, Ortega's Nicaragua, and other revolutionary regimes in underdeveloped countries.[120] It is ironic that many such intellectuals think of themselves as followers of Marx, who insisted that socialism would be a necessary consequence, and therefore only a sequel, of advanced industrial capitalism.[121]

In the late nineteenth and early twentieth centuries, some intellectuals and many workers in Western Europe had come to expect a socialist proletarian revolution. Disgusted with the failure of their socialist parties to make such a revolution, they wanted to associate themselves with a successful revolution that claimed to be proletarian and socialist. Thus, some of those who desired a workers' revolution in the West were attracted to think of themselves as Leninists by the fact that Lenin inaccurately described his revolution in Marxian terms as one of workers and by the fact that his myth was supported by the role played in the revolution by real workers.

The resulting identification of Marxism with Leninism was reinforced in two ways: Lenin and his comrades in the new Soviet regime, believing that they had made a workers' revolution, thought they needed, and expected, the support of workers in the West. They therefore labeled the new Communist parties, which did support the Soviet regime, both Marxist and Leninist.

These same labels were applied to the Communists by their opponents on the political Right. By having them linked to the Soviet regime, they could be discredited as alien and unpatriotic and as proponents of policies being pursued in the Soviet Union. Both Communists and conservatives in the West, then, as well as the Soviet government and its Third International had an interest in believing that Marxism and Leninism were the same thing; and, by proclaiming it, each of them confirmed in the minds of the others that this was, indeed, the case.

The Beginnings of the Confusion

Clearly, there have been many people in all parts of the world and since the Russian Revolution who have had the personal and larger political need to see Marxism and Leninism as a single ideology and to ignore the obvious differences between them. But historically the identification of the two ideologies goes back to the fact that Lenin and his small group of supporters had considered themselves Marxists. Why, then, did Lenin and his comrades, even when they argued with the Mensheviks and when they finally broke openly with the social-democratic Marxism of the Second International in 1914 and still more drastically in 1917, not recognize that theirs was and always had been a different ideology and why did their social-democratic antagonists not recognize it?

Violently as the two sides denounced each other, they never questioned that both of them were or had been Marxists. They explained their differences as resulting from their antagonists' misinterpretations and distortions of Marx's doctrine, from their failure to understand and act upon a common theory, and, above all, from betrayal and "renegadism"—in brief, as due to intellectual and moral shortcomings of those they disagreed with. Though they were, of course, aware of differences between the Russian and the West European environments, they did not ascribe their ideological differences primarily to them. They had all studied their Marx and fired quotations from his writings at each other, but they forgot that, according to him, different socioeconomic conditions should produce different ideologies, and they believed that the same Marxism could flourish in Holland and Bulgaria and, above all, in Germany and Russia.

As far as Lenin and the Bolsheviks are concerned, the question of why they saw themselves as Marxists probably can be answered quite simply. They had joined the Russian Marxian movement and they were committed revolutionaries. As Marxists in the West and especially in the SPD also proclaimed their commitment to revolutionary principles, the Bolsheviks could easily assume that they themselves, too, were Marxists. They probably could not, and certainly did not, want to see that the word "revolution" could have different meanings in different environments.

Once committed to what they regarded as Marxism, Lenin and the other Bolsheviks, like most people and certainly like most politicians, very probably believed, and surely wanted others to believe, that they remained consistent and faithful to their principles. If they felt good about themselves and thought they gained politically by asserting their consistent Marxism, they could, by the same token, weaken their Marxist opponents by accusing them of being renegades. That, as Leninists, they themselves were not Marxists simply did not and could not occur to them. It was only after Lenin's death that Leninists came sometimes to refer to their ideology not simply as Marxism but as Marxism-Leninism, thus suggesting that Lenin had added something to Marxism, but presumably something wholly consistent with it.

If Lenin and the early Leninists had an obvious interest in thinking of themselves as Marxists, why did their Marxist opponents not clearly dispute their claim to that label? Why did they at most argue that Leninists had abandoned Marxism, but not that Leninists had never been Marxists? Here, one must first recall that, before World War I, the line between Leninism and Marxism had not been as clearly drawn as it was later and as I have sought to draw it here. The issues in the conflicts between Bolsheviks and Mensheviks had not been well defined and had often seemed to involve mostly organizational questions and even Lenin's personal style of leadership. To Marxists in the West, these conflicts remained largely incomprehensible and appeared to be a peculiarly Russian phenomenon, perhaps to be explained by the conditions of illegality and secrecy in which Russian Marxists and Leninists had to function. Since, apart from some possible parallels in the Balkans, Leninism was, in fact, still a uniquely Russian phenomenon, there was no way they could see it as a distinct ideology, as we can now see it in retrospect.

It is also worth recalling that the Russian Social-Democratic Party, including its Bolshevik wing, was regarded, both in the West and in Russia, as part of an international labor movement. Different as it was organizationally from the Western social-democratic parties, it was, until World War I, linked to them in the Second International. What is more, the leaders and ideologists of all these parties, including the Russians, many of whom spent years in exile in Western Europe, read each others' writings, met frequently, and talked to each other. Since they used the same words, they believed that they meant the same things, that they stood for the same interests, fighting the same enemies. No doubt all of them, but particularly the Russians, who represented a weak party, wanted to believe it, because they derived a feeling of strength and confidence from their association with a large international movement.

When these personal and organizational links were finally broken, as Communist parties seceded from socialist ones and the Third International was formed in opposition to the Second, and when the differences between the two sides became very clear, neither could revise its past views and admit that it had been mistaken in believing that both adhered to the same ideology. Each could accuse the other of betraying and abandoning Marxism, but neither questioned that the other had once been Marxist. Traitors and renegades, after all, must be former comrades.

Another factor contributing to Marxists' and Leninists' belief, especially in the first few decades of the twentieth century, that they shared or had shared the same ideology may have been their conception of ideology. Marx had argued that different classes have different ideologies, at least when they become class-conscious. There was some capitalism in Russia and there were some workers, and it was taken for granted by Marxists and early Leninists alike that these would grow in strength. Lenin's belief that he represented Russian workers, which was neither wholly unreasonable nor even wholly wrong, could be accepted by those who represented Western workers, and it seemed to follow to both Marxists and Leninists that, representing the same class, they held the same ideology.

There is, however, also the question of the extent to which they regarded their ideologies as ideologies at all. Marxists and the early Leninists who were educated as Marxists were keenly aware of other people's views being conditioned by their social position, but, like everyone else, they believed that their own views were simply true. They saw their Marxism or what they regarded as their Marxism as the ideology of the proletariat in the sense that it would appeal to the proletariat rather than to other classes, but to them it was not a class-bound ideology; it was objectively true, that is, it was science. Now while there can and even must be different ideologies in industrial Germany and agrarian Russia, because there are different classes, there can be only one physics and one biology and, similarly, only one Marxism. This view, too, surely contributed to the belief in the identity of Marxism and Leninism.

EUROCENTRISM

Russia: A European Country

Lenin and the early Leninists on the one hand and their Marxist antagonists in Russia and in the West on the other could not see Leninism and Marxism as different ideologies, as I do, because the perspective that allows me to distinguish the two was not available to them. This perspective, which sees the world as divided broadly into two types of societies, one industrialized and the other nonindustrialized, each type with its own pattern of political change, developed only in the second half of the twentieth century and has, in one form or another, been widely accepted as analytically useful.

Before World War I, in the period of concern to us here, continental European intellectuals saw the world as divided differently. On the one hand, there was Europe and also the countries settled by Europeans, especially in North America; this was thought of as the civilized world. On the other hand, there was the rest of the world, presumably uncivilized. About its societies, even highly educated and sophisticated intellectuals, apart from a few specialists and adventurous travelers and explorers, knew and cared very little.[122]

One difference between the two views of the world—industrial and nonindustrial on the one hand, European and non-European on the other—is crucial in our context. In the former view, tsarist Russia is separated from Western and Central Europe and analytically linked to underdeveloped Asia, Africa, and Latin America; in the latter view, it is linked to the rest of Europe. Before World War I, Russia was generally regarded as a European country, different but not wholly different, from Western Europe and certainly not from the two big military-bureaucratic empires of Central Europe.

No geographical feature clearly divides Europe and Asia, nor does any political boundary separate them. Mongol and Turkic people from Asia moved into and occupied or ruled parts of Europe and, in more recent centuries down to the present, Russia and Turkey have consisted of territories on both continents. Still, by the nineteenth century, Russia was clearly a European country. Its rulers and armies had long been involved in European politics; it was, like some other European countries, Christian and Slavic; its intellectuals were imbued with Western culture and values; its scientists, writers, and musicians made major contributions to European science, literature, and music.

By the late nineteenth century, Russian industrialization, much of it financed by Western European capital, was rapidly progressing, linking Russia even more to the rest of Europe and making it more like the rest of Europe. All this was taken for granted by intellectuals in the West, at a time when the non-European world, with the possible exception of

North America, was still largely ignored by them. Russia's peasants, nine-tenths of its population, may have had more in common with Chinese and Indian than with French and German peasants, but it was unthinkable for Western and Russian intellectuals to link in their minds a country where men had light skins and wore proper Western suits or uniforms with countries where they had darker skins and wore pigtails, turbans, or loincloths. Russia was in Europe and therefore assumed to be understandable; the rest of the world was far away and very strange and, no doubt for that reason, was held to be, at least vaguely, inferior.[123]

Marxism: A Eurocentric View of History

Western Marxists and Russian Marxists and would-be Marxists were at least as Eurocentric in their outlook as other European intellectuals. They, too, paid little attention to the history and politics of non-European countries, not only because they had little relevant factual knowledge but also because the Marxian categories with which they operated were ill-suited for gathering and organizing such knowledge.

To be sure, Marx's materialist conception of history seeks to provide a very general framework for an explanation of all human history with its conception of the forces of production and, corresponding to them, the relations of production or property relations constituting a base on which rises a legal, political, and ideological superstructure. But even the assumption of this scheme that the forces of production are a dynamic element, which is thus ultimately responsible for all change in history, is derived from certain phases of European history. It does not in fact apply to traditional aristocratic empires, where the forces and hence the relations of production and with them the political and ideological superstructure may, sometimes for millennia, remain stable.[124]

The progressive stages of history and modes of production—notably the feudal, the bourgeois, and the future socialist one, which Marx saw as growing out of the tensions between the dynamic forces of production and the conservative property relations and out of the conflict between the classes associated with these—are clearly derived from his view of European history. He envisaged a pattern of history according to which a bourgeoisie evolves under aristocratic rule and replaces the latter through a bourgeois revolution. It then develops capitalist industry to such an extent that the new industrial working class becomes numerous and powerful enough to replace bourgeois rule and introduce socialism.

At a time when, to European intellectuals, history effectively meant European history, Marxists vaguely assumed, when they thought of the non-European world at all, that these stages of history applied to it, too. It is only more recently, mostly in the second half of the twentieth century, that it has become quite evident that the pattern outlined by

Marx could be seen as valid, if at all, only in Western Europe, at best as partially valid in Central Europe, and not at all valid in Eastern Europe and the rest of the underdeveloped world.

Marx himself, perhaps because, unlike his future followers, he lived in England with its extensive commercial and colonial contacts in Asia, had some doubts about the universal validity of his scheme of stages of history. In some suggestive passages, he introduced the concept of an "Asiatic mode of production" that does not fit into this scheme but, being overwhelmingly concerned with past and future European history, he never developed this concept systematically. While Marx thought of the Asiatic mode of production and of "Oriental despotism" mostly in connection with China and India, Plekhanov applied these concepts to past Russian history, too. But, like Marxists in the West, he came to assume that modern Russia would follow the course of Western European history.

Generally Marxists and would-be Marxists in Russia and in the West, being Eurocentric, showed little interest in Marx's Asiatic mode of production. They thought of Russian history as European, because they had no other way of thinking of it, and conceptualized Russia's past and especially its future in terms of the Europe-oriented Marxian stages of feudal, bourgeois-capitalist, and proletarian-socialist predominance. This was true even of those, including Lenin, who sometimes referred to Russia as "semi-Asiatic," for they had no non-European paradigm by which to understand Asia.

To be sure, Marxists and early Leninists were not quite comfortable in applying the scheme of the feudal, capitalist, and socialist stages to Russia, for most of them had little faith in the willingness or ability of the Russian bourgeoisie to overthrow the tsarist regime and replace it with a "bourgeois-democratic" one. After all, even the German and Austrian bourgeoisies had not successfully attacked and replaced their monarchical regimes. Still, so wedded were they to Marxian concepts that they were convinced that there had to be a bourgeois revolution even if there was no revolutionary bourgeoisie to make one.

Thus, until 1917 there were extensive debates and disagreements among Marxists and Leninists as to who would make the bourgeois revolution. Lenin, as we have seen, made his Party, that is, revolutionary intellectuals, with its presumed proletarian following the active revolutionary force, but to make the "bourgeois-democratic" revolution, it would rely heavily on the peasantry. Trotsky thought that what might begin as a bourgeois revolution would, through a "permanent revolution" and with the support of the Western proletariat, turn immediately and without an intervening capitalist stage into a proletarian revolution and result in the establishment of a dictatorship of the proletariat. The

Mensheviks hoped for a bourgeois revolution but thought that the working class would have to play a major role in it, even before it grew powerful in the subsequent capitalist and democratic stage. Kautsky suggested that the inevitable bourgeois revolution would have to be made by the proletariat allied with the peasantry. It was only when Lenin saw his chance to take power that he effectively decided to skip the bourgeois revolution altogether and to call his revolution a socialist proletarian one.

While there were disagreements among both Marxists and Leninists on just what stage of history Russia was in, on problems of the transition from each stage to the next, and on the role of the various classes, none of them questioned the relevance to Russian history of the European concepts of feudal, bourgeois, and proletarian stages. In their thinking on Russia, they put tremendous emphasis on two relatively small and weak classes, the industrial bourgeoisie and the industrial working class, because these had come to play major roles in Western European politics. Russia, however, was overwhelmingly agrarian, the great majority of its population consisted of peasants, and the major active contestants in its politics consisted, on the one hand, of the overlapping old aristocratic ruling groups of the tsarist court, the landowners, the bureaucracy, the military, and the Orthodox Church and, on the other, the revolutionary intelligentsia. Lenin did adjust his thinking to this reality of Russian underdevelopment and thereby replaced Marxism with Leninism, but he concealed this adjustment and replacement from himself and from Marxists in Western Europe by his use of Marxian terminology.

Having only European history available as a model of historical development, the Eurocentric Marxists expected Russia to develop as Western Europe had, just as, in more recent decades, Eurocentric intellectuals, including American ones, have often, more or less explicitly, thought of underdeveloped countries as merely "behind" the West in a process of "political development" or "Westernization." In particular, Marxists and Leninists regarded the Russian revolutionary movement as a European revolutionary movement. Before, during, and after the Russian Revolution, parallels were constantly drawn with the French Revolution, that is, the great bourgeois revolution, and the Paris Commune, supposedly the first proletarian revolution.[125] Who and what in the Russian Revolution represented Jacobinism, Thermidorianism, and Bonapartism were widely debated among Marxists and Leninists.[126]

Ignorance and Indifference

It is not surprising that people who could think only in European terms accepted the Marxian words of Lenin as Marxian substance. Being unfamiliar with the revolutionary politics of underdeveloped countries, they had no way of understanding Leninism as a distinct ideology characteristic of such politics.

At the time, this was inevitable, because no pattern of revolutionary politics in underdeveloped countries had yet emerged. The modernizing, anticolonial and antitraditional revolutionary movements, with which we have become so familiar in the second half of the twentieth century, were mostly unborn or in their infancy and could be only dimly recognized. Lenin could not yet be compared with Mao or Nehru, Ho or Sukarno in East and South Asia; Mossadegh, Nasser, or Ben Bella in the Middle East and North Africa; Nkrumah, Touré, or Nyerere in Africa south of the Sahara; Paz, Castro, or Ortega in Latin America, to name but some of the more prominent leaders of modernizing movements to emerge after World War I and mostly only after World War II.

It is also true, though, that Marxists and early Leninists, because of their Eurocentrism, paid very little attention to the underdeveloped world, even when revolutionary events did occur there or were foreseeable. The Socialist International, at its 1896 (London), 1900 (Paris), and especially its 1904 (Amsterdam) and 1907 (Stuttgart) congresses, held debates and passed resolutions on the colonial question, but these were primarily concerned with the socialist parties' attitude toward the colonial policies of Western European governments and hardly with the nature and prospects of the colonial societies. *Die Neue Zeit*, the outstanding Marxist international journal of its time, published a total of only about twenty-five articles on the domestic politics of underdeveloped countries other than Russia in the more than three decades from it establishment in 1883 to the outbreak of World War I.[127] In the same period, it published over 170 articles on Russia. No wonder Marxists were predisposed to see Lenin in a European light (whether as a Robespierre, a Blanqui, or a Bebel) and Leninism as Marxism.

Lenin himself wrote virtually nothing on what he usually called the "East" until 1908, the one exception being an article concerned with the effects of the Boxer Rebellion on Russia and its working class.[128] It took up 6 pages out of the approximately 7,000 pages of Lenin's writings from 1893 to 1907 (in the first 14 volumes of his *Collected Works*). In two brief articles in 1908,[129] Lenin commented sympathetically but hardly analytically on revolutionary upheavals in Persia, Turkey, China, and India, and beginning in July 1912 he reacted in two short articles[130] to the Chinese Revolution that had broken out in the preceding year. He linked these Asian revolutions to the Russian Revolution of 1905 but, far from thereby associating Russia with the underdeveloped world, he reached the conclusion "that the East has definitely taken the Western path, that new *hundreds of millions* of people will from now on share in the struggle for the ideals which the West has already worked out for itself."[131]

To the extent that domestic politics in underdeveloped countries is analyzed by Lenin at all, it is by the application of Marxian class categories. Revolutions in these countries are designated as "bourgeois," but, as he had in
Russia, Lenin links or even identifies the bourgeoisie, in a quite un-Marxian
manner, with the peasantry. Thus, he says: "The chief representative, or the
chief social bulwark, of this Asian bourgeoisie that is still capable of supporting a historically progressive cause, is the peasant."[132]

One reason why European Marxists and Leninists paid so little attention to the non-European world is no doubt that, keenly aware of political
and social change in Europe, they had the impression that there was
little or no change in the rest of the world. But only extreme Eurocentrism
can account for the fact that Lenin would, between 1911 and 1917, when
he wrote hundreds of articles, devote only two brief pieces totaling eight
pages and a very few scattered remarks elsewhere to the Chinese Revolution, one of the great revolutions that brought down one of the
longest-lasting empires in history. *Die Neue Zeit* under Kautsky's edi-
torship published two substantial articles analyzing the Chinese Revolution,[133] but Kautsky himself wrote nothing on the subject at the time.

However slightly, Lenin at least reacted to the Chinese Revolution.
The Mexican Revolution was evidently totally ignored by him. If he was
aware of it at all, he must have considered it irrelevant to his interests.
In retrospect, it seems truly amazing that "a man who for twenty-four
hours of the day is taken up with the revolution, who has no other
thoughts but thoughts of revolution, and who, even in his sleep, dreams
of nothing but revolution," as Pavel Axelrod said of Lenin,[134] would
have no comment at all, from its outbreak in 1910 until his death in 1924,
on one of the greatest revolutions in history, a massive upheaval that
lasted ten years and cost about a million lives.[135] *Die Neue Zeit* published
one article on the Mexican Revolution,[136] but Kautsky, Rosa Luxemburg,
Trotsky, and Gramsci,[137] and probably most contemporary European
Marxists, similarly paid no attention to it.

It is a fascinating fact that both Marxists and Leninists, who were so
concerned with the phenomenon of revolution and eagerly analyzed the
prospects for revolutions in Europe, showed no or very little interest
when two huge revolutions occurred. No doubt, they were not very
well informed about events in China and Mexico, but their minimal
reactions prove that they were not wholly ignorant of them—the three
articles in *Die Neue Zeit* alone provided quite a bit of information—and
they could surely have learned more had they really pursued the matter.

One cannot help concluding that, before World War I, Marxists and
Leninists had generally not only little knowledge of but also little interest
in the world outside Europe. It must have seemed to them quite irrelevant to their concerns. As late as July 1916, Lenin could write: "A blow
delivered against the power of the English imperialist bourgeoisie by a

rebellion in Ireland is a hundred times more significant than a blow of equal force delivered in Asia or Africa."[138] Both Marxists and Leninists thought of the non-European world, if at all, mostly as an object of colonialism; and its people, often described indiscriminately as "the natives," were not political actors to them. If they considered the domestic politics of underdeveloped, non-European countries at all, they tended to use Marxian class categories in their analyses—or substitute them for analysis—putting special emphasis on the least relevant ones, the bourgeoisie and the proletariat.

No More Excuse for Eurocentrism

Marxists, being interested in the prospects for the working class coming to power in industrialized countries, could at least, quite rightly, feel that nothing happening in underdeveloped countries, like China and Mexico, could be relevant as a model for them. Leninists did not even have that excuse. It was only the Eurocentrism and the Marxian language they shared with the Marxists that kept them from seeing the relevance of revolutions in underdeveloped countries to their concern with a revolution in Russia.

Lenin could identify with Bebel and, until 1914, Kautsky, the principal leader and the principal theoretician of the Marxist labor movement in Wilhemine Germany, because he considered himself a proletarian revolutionary leader. He could not identify with Sun Yat-sen, whom he considered a bourgeois revolutionary.[139] In fact, in Russia and in China and in underdeveloped countries generally, the Bebels and Kautskys, if they have existed at all, have not come to power. There have been no proletarian revolutions there and no bourgeois ones either. There have been modernizing revolutions led by intellectuals like Lenin and Sun; and Lenin's role in history, though not his vocabulary, is much closer to that of Sun than that of Bebel or Kautsky.

Revolutions like the Chinese and the Mexican ones can generally be described as directed against traditional regimes recently modified by modernization from without, revolutions led by men inspired by modern Western ideologies and gaining mass support in an impoverished peasantry and a small class of former peasants radicalized by having recently been turned into workers. That description fits the Russian Revolution, too, and Leninism is, as I have tried to show, precisely a response to the situation it refers to.

With their view of history essentially confined to Europe and with what little they knew of the non-European world cast in terms of European history, pre–World War I Marxists and Leninists could not see the Russian Revolution—either the one of 1905 or the coming one of 1917—in the light of revolutions in underdeveloped countries. It evidently never occurred to them that the long-drawn-out, confusing events of the Chinese and Mexican revolutions could turn out to be models for European Russia. The many other revolutions in underdeveloped countries, beginning with the one in Turkey, that have opened up this perspective to us did not occur until after World War I.

Under these circumstances, it was all but impossible for both Marxists and Leninists before World War I to link Leninism to the politics of underdevelopment and thus to distinguish it from Marxism. That Marxists and Leninists themselves failed to do this has, not surprisingly, helped to mislead most analysts down to the present to identify Leninism with Marxism.

The confusion of Leninism with Marxism may have been excusable and even inevitable before World War I, and then it became useful for quite different interests to maintain that confusion. Those with deep emotional commitments to certain symbols—perhaps mostly some Communists and some anti-Communists—may even now need to perpetuate the identification of Marxism and Leninism. But for most people with any scholarly interest in the subject, there seems for some time now to have been no good reason for confusing two such different ideologies. To suggest that the German Social-Democratic Party, on the one hand, and the Ethiopian Workers Party or the Congolese Labor Party, on the other, have some common background or that the study of one will provide an understanding of the other seems manifestly nonsensical.

Even Eurocentric Lenin began to look to the "East" for revolutions to occur when he was disappointed by the failure of revolutions in the West to follow his own revolution. In one of his last pieces of writing, he recognized clearly, if only halfheartedly and hesitatingly, that the Russian Revolution had something in common with revolutions in underdeveloped countries that distinguished it from Western European revolutions:

Because Russia stands on the border-line between the civilised countries and . . . all the Oriental, non-European countries, she could and was, indeed, bound to reveal certain distinguishing features; although these, of course, are in keeping with the general line of world development, they distinguish her revolution from those which took place in the West-European countries and introduce certain partial innovations as the revolution moves on to the countries of the East.[140]

Of course Lenin could not, or at least not explicitly, admit that Leninism must therefore also be distinguished from Marxism; but if he himself could come at all close to recognizing this, we should have no difficulty doing so.

Lenin concludes his remarkable article with these words:

It need hardly be said that a textbook written on Kautskian lines was a very useful thing in its day. But it is time, for all that, to abandon the idea that it foresaw all the forms of development of subsequent world history. It would be timely to say that those who think so are simply fools.[141]

If by "a textbook written on Kautskian lines" Lenin refers to Karl Kautsky's and other Marxists'—and, indeed, also his own—Eurocentric views, he is quite right. Having gone in the opposite direction by interpreting Lenin as an ideologist of the non-European or, rather, the nonindustrial, world, and therefore as a Leninist rather than a Marxist, I hope that the John Kautskian lines expressed in this essay will not deserve similarly harsh comments.

Notes

1. In Peru, "Abimael Guzmán Reynoso . . . who founded and leads the Shining Path . . . bills himself as 'The Fourth Sword of Marxism' " after Marx, Lenin, and Mao. *New York Times*, April 7, 1992, A6. As but one of innumerable examples of the loose use of the term "Marxism," one may cite the *New York Times*, December 28, 1989, 7, which, reporting on warfare in Ethiopia, referred to Colonel Mengistu as "one of the most hard-line Marxist rulers left in the world" and to the Tigrean People's Liberation Front as seeking to "replace him with its more rigid version of Marxism-Leninism," while "the other major rebel group, the Eritrean People's Liberation Front . . . is also Marxist."

2. As an approach to social analysis—a matter I do not deal with here—Marxism has for a century remained stimulating and influential in different areas of social science and is, in this sense, alive or at least not dead.

3. In the post-Communist era, some of those in the former Soviet Union and in Eastern Europe who feel that they lost political power, supported by some of those who feel materially worse off or are nostalgic for their former security, may express their opposition to the new order by employing Leninist symbols. To the extent that that new order is being justified in terms of the symbols of capitalism, Lenin's Marxist anticapitalist symbols lend themselves well to that purpose. In fact, however, such a revival of Marxist and Leninist symbols, perhaps in defense of the interests of present and former bureaucrats and technocrats, has nothing to do with a revival either of laborite Marxism or of modernizing Leninism, as I shall define them in this essay.

4. In late 1991, in an interview with an East German newspaper, the chairman of the Social-Democratic parliamentary caucus in Bonn said that the SPD should "review its terminology" and stop using the word "socialism." *This Week in Germany* (New York), December 20, 1991, 2.

5. My concept of ideology is what Martin Seliger calls an "inclusive" one. It "covers sets of factual and moral propositions which serve to posit, explain

and justify ends and means of organized social action, especially political action, irrespective of whether such action aims to preserve, amend, destroy or rebuild any given order." Martin Seliger, *The Marxist Conception of Ideology* (Cambridge: Cambridge University Press, 1977), 1. See also Martin Seliger, *Ideology and Politics* (London: Allen and Unwin, 1976).

6. Marx did produce some significant writings relevant to these problems, conveniently collected in Shlomo Avinieri, ed., *Karl Marx on Colonialism and Modernization* (Garden City, N.Y.: Doubleday, 1968); Karl Marx and Frederick Engels, *On Colonialism* (New York: International Publishers, 1972); Karl Marx, *Pre-Capitalist Economic Formations* (New York: International Publishers, 1965). His insights in this area, notably his concepts of Oriental despotism and the Asiatic mode of production, are, however, marginal to the main body of his thought and had little influence on Leninism.

7. For a careful study of Engels' relation with the early German, Austrian, French, and Italian socialist parties, see Gary P. Steenson, *After Marx, Before Lenin. Marxism and Socialist Working-Class Parties in Europe, 1884–1914* (Pittsburgh: University of Pittsburgh Press, 1991).

8. That term refers to such writers as Lukács, Korsch, Gramsci, Marcuse, Sartre, and members of the Frankfurt School, all marginal to or outside the mainstream of the development of Western European Social-Democratic thought, in whose hands "Marxism became a type of theory in certain critical respects quite distinct from anything that had preceded it." Perry Anderson, *Considerations on Western Marxism* (London: NLB, 1976), 25. See also Gareth Stedman Jones, *Western Marxism. A Critical Reader* (London: NLB, 1977); Ben Agger, *Western Marxism. An Introduction* (Santa Monica, Calif.: Goodyear, 1979); Russell Jacoby, *Dialectic of Defeat: Contours of Western Marxism* (Cambridge: Cambridge University Press, 1981).

9. John Plamenatz says of Lenin that he repeated Marx's "phrases and hurled them at his enemies; they passed so often through his mind and came so readily to his pen that it never occurred to him that he did not understand them. They were familiar to him; and, being a simple man, he made the mistake of thinking that what is familiar is understood." John Plamenatz, *German Marxism and Russian Communism* (New York: Harper & Row, 1965), 250. One need not think of Lenin as "a simple man" to appreciate why Marx's phrases were so familiar to him, yet not understood by him. His dual environment can account for both: On the one hand, he moved in Marxist circles, read Marxist literature, engaged in polemics with Marxists. On the other hand, he wanted to be, and turned out to be, an effective revolutionary politician in an underdeveloped country; as such, he could not afford to "understand" the Marxian phrases in their original meaning.

10. That Lenin's Marxian vocabulary expresses an ideology different from Marxism is indicated by the fact that Leninist modernizing movements and regimes, like those in Russia, China, Vietnam, and Cuba, are, in some respects, remarkably similar to non-Leninist modernizing ones that do not employ the Marxian terminology, like those in Mexico, India, Algeria, and Egypt.

In my "Comparative Communism Versus Comparative Politics," *Studies in Comparative Communism* 6, nos. 1 and 2 (Spring/Summer 1973): 135–70, I attempted to demonstrate that all Communist regimes, just because they are

Communist, are not alike or different from all non-Communist ones. In my *Patterns of Modernizing Revolutions: Mexico and the Soviet Union*, Sage Professional Papers in Comparative Politics, 5 (Beverly Hills, Calif.: Sage, 1975), I elaborated on similarities in the prerevolutionary, revolutionary, and postrevolutionary development of Mexico and Russia.

11. An Austrian Socialist writes about his Party in the 1920s: "Almost every field of activity of the individual was integrated in the Party. Cyclists and lovers of music, amateur botanists, chess-players and mountaineers, bird-fanciers, football players, wrestlers, and singers formed groups of their own within the movement. Tens of thousands of children belonged to the groups of 'Children's Friends' and 'Red Falcons'. . . . The Socialists had hundreds of their own libraries. They had their own study groups in sociology, psychology, literature and philosophy. . . . They hired trains and chartered ships to go on holiday in far-away countries." Julius Braunthal, *In Search of the Millennium* (London: Gollancz, 1945), 253–54. There was also the Federation of Freethinkers and the (smaller) Federation of Religious (i.e., Catholic) Socialists, the Workers' League of Abstainers (from alcohol), and the Workers' Association "Flame" (advocating and practicing cremation). These and numerous other working-class organizations were represented in the exhibition "Mit uns zieht die neue Zeit. Arbeiterkultur in Oesterreich, 1918–1934," in Vienna in 1981.

For a good brief description of the Social-Democratic working-class subculture in one small German town in the Weimar period, see William Sheridan Allen, *The Nazi Seizure of Power* (New York: New Viewpoints, 1973), 15–16. For a careful study of German labor movement associations, their club life and festivals, songs, poetry, drama, and educational activities, see Vernon L. Lidtke, *The Alternative Culture. Socialist Labor in Imperial Germany* (New York: Oxford University Press, 1985). See also Richard J. Evans, "Introduction: The Sociological Interpretation of German Labour History," in Richard J. Evans, ed., *The German Working Class, 1888–1933* (London: Croom Helm, 1982), 19.

12. For a detailed account of bureaucratic and legal obstructionism and police harassment of Social Democrats, see Alex Hall, *Scandal, Sensation and Social Democracy* (Cambridge: Cambridge University Press, 1977), 41–112, 120–42. See also W. L. Guttsman, *The German Social Democratic Party, 1875–1933. From Ghetto to Government* (London: Allen and Unwin, 1981), 132–41.

13. Quoted in Dieter Groh, *Negative Integration und revolutionärer Attentismus. Die deutsche Sozialdemokratie am Vorabend des ersten Weltkrieges* (Frankfurt am Main: Ullstein-Propyläen, 1973), 37–38. See also Hall, *Scandal*, 119.

14. In 1874, when there were, on the average, about 21,000 eligible voters in each of 397 electoral districts, there were 44 districts with fewer than 16,000 eligible voters and only 9 with more than 32,000. In 1912, however, when, on the average, there were about 36,000 eligible voters in each district, there were 97 districts with fewer than 24,000 voters and 32 with more than 60,000, 2 of them with more than 200,000. Gerhard A. Ritter, *Wahlgeschichtliches Arbeitsbuch* (Munich: Beck, 1980), 98. See also Stanley Suval, *Electoral Politics in Wilhemine Germany* (Chapel Hill: University of North Carolina Press, 1985), 229; Bernhard Vogel, Dieter Nohlen, and Rainer-Olaf Schultze, *Wahlen in Deutschland* (Berlin: de Gruyter, 1971), 99–100; and Max Schwarz, ed., *M.d.R. Biographisches Handbuch der Reichstage* (Hannover: Verlag für Literatur und Zeitgeschichte, 1965), 123.

15. These figures are computed from tables in Vogel et al., *Wahlen*, 290–93.

16. The SPD did not participate in the elections for the Prussian parliament through 1898. In the elections of 1903, 1908, and 1913, the conservatives and the Social Democrats won the percentages of the popular vote and of seats shown below.

	Conservatives		Free Conservatives		Total Conservatives		Social-Democrats	
	vote	seats	vote	seats	vote	seats	vote	seats
03	19.39	33.03	2.87	13.86	22.26	46.89	18.79	0
08	14.15	34.31	2.54	13.54	16.69	47.85	23.87	1.58
13	14.75	33.41	2.00	12.19	16.75	45.60	28.38	2.26

Source: Ritter, *Wahlgeschichtliches Arbeitsbuch*, 146–47.

17. This is emphasized in Lidtke, *The Alternative Culture*, 3–6.

18. "Someday the worker must seize political power in order to build up the new organization of labor. . . . But we have not asserted that the ways to achieve that goal are everywhere the same." From a speech by Marx at Amsterdam, September 8, 1872, in Robert C. Tucker, ed., *The Marx-Engels Reader* (2d ed., New York: W. W. Norton, 1978), 523.

19. On the extent to which Bismarck and his successors considered a coup d'état because of their fear and loathing of the Social Democrats, see Guenther Roth, *The Social Democrats in Imperial Germany* (Totowa, N.J.: Bedminister Press, 1963), 67–84; and the German works on the subject cited in Hall, *Scandal*, 201, n. 23. In a letter of 1888 to the future Emperor William II, Bismarck quoted with approval the old rhyme "Gegen Demokraten helfen nur Soldaten" (against democrats, only soldiers are effective); Roth, *The Social Democrats*, 78. In 1910, Elard von Oldenburg-Januschau, the leader in the Prussian House of Representatives of the Conservatives, the largest party, said in the Reichstag: "The King of Prussia and German Emperor must be able at any moment to say to a lieutenant: 'Take ten men and shut the Reichstag down.' " Elard von Oldenburg-Januschau, *Erinnerungen* (Leipzig: Koehler & Amelang, 1936), 110. Schorske quotes this statement but, evidently misreading the German *schliessen* as *schiessen*, translates the emperor's order as "shoot the Reichstag." Carl F. Schorske, *German Social Democracy, 1905–1917* (Cambridge, Mass.: Harvard University Press, 1955), 168.

20. " 'Revolution' and 'revolutionary' . . . tended to become a slogan and an attitude of mind, an expression of the antagonism to the existing society rather than a method to be employed to bring about radical change." Guttsman, *The German Social Democratic Party*, 72.

21. The peasantry in Germany was, of course, very different in its status and attitudes from the peasantries Leninists had to deal with, as we shall see in chapter 3. Collaboration of the SPD with other parties and reformism were strongest in the three southern states of the German Empire, where urbanization

and industrialization, especially with respect to heavy industry, were least advanced, the Catholic Church was strong, and the SPD was relatively weak.

22. Bernstein wrote in 1899 that those opponents of Social Democracy who recognized that political concessions must be made to it would be much more influential "if the social democracy could find the courage to emancipate itself from a phraseology which is actually outworn and if it would make up its mind to appear what it is in reality to-day, a democratic, socialistic party of reform." Eduard Bernstein, *Evolutionary Socialism* (New York: Schocken Books, 1961), 197.

23. That it was not just the leadership and the intellectuals, but the rank-and-file members (at least in some areas), to whom the emphasis on revolution appealed is an important conclusion reached by a study of local SPD history: "Düsseldorf, like Berlin, found the Kautskyan synthesis of revolutionary theory, reformist tactics and isolation appealing . . . because it offered an analysis of and means to deal with the ambiguous, stalemated society that was Imperial Germany." Mary Nolan, *Social Democracy and Society. Working-Class Radicalism in Düsseldorf, 1890–1920* (Cambridge: Cambridge University Press, 1981), 89.

24. Bernstein's statement, to which he referred in *Evolutionary Socialism*, 202, is rarely quoted in full. It reads as follows: "I openly confess that I have exceedingly little sympathy for and interest in what is commonly thought of as the 'final goal of socialism.' That goal, whatever it may be, is nothing at all to me, the movement is everything. And by movement, I mean both the general movement of society, i.e., social progress, and the political and economic agitation and organization to bring about this progress." Eduard Bernstein, "Der Kampf der Sozialdemokratie und die Revolution der Gesellschaft," *Die Neue Zeit* 16/1 (1898): 556.

25. Victor Adler, "Der Dresdener Parteitag," *Arbeiter-Zeitung* (Vienna), September 13, 1903, reprinted in *Aufsätze, Reden und Briefe* (Vienna: Wiener Volksbuchhandlung, 1929), vol. VI, pt. 1, 253. Otto Bauer, the Social-Democratic leader in the First Austrian Republic, said of Adler: "It was a thought he often repeated that one could bear the difficult duties of day-to-day work only if one's eyes remained fixed on the great, inspiring historical future goal." Otto Bauer, "Einleitung," ibid., xxxiii. And the British socialist Brailsford wrote of the Austrian Social Democrats: "Behind their day to day politics they had a view of life and a conception of the meaning and processes of history which inspired all their thinking and gave them even in misfortune and defeat an enviable serenity and the assurance of ultimate victory. This Marxist interpretation of history gave them the same sense that destiny was behind them in their struggles, which the invincible Puritans of the Commonwealth possessed, because they trusted the promises of God." H. N. Brailsford, "Introduction" to Braunthal, *In Search of the Millennium*, 9.

It is interesting to note that Kautsky, Bernstein's principal opponent in the debate about Revisionism, stated quite explicitly that the function of the "final goal" was to maintain the unity of the labor movement in the face of both the tendency of its specialized branches to pursue their tasks as ends in themselves and divisions caused by those who, in response to changing conditions, accuse the Party of being too moderate or too radical. Karl Kautsky, "Die Revision des Programms der Sozialdemokratie in Oesterreich," *Die Neue Zeit* 20/1 (1901): 69–70.

26. Roth, *The Social Democrats*, 318.

27. In several earlier books and articles, I have dealt with the politics of modernization in underdeveloped countries and the role of intellectuals in it. See particularly my *The Political Consequences of Modernization* (New York: John Wiley, 1972; reprint, Huntington, NY: Krieger, 1980) and *Communism and the Politics of Development* (New York: John Wiley, 1968). Some of the next few paragraphs rest in good part on what I discussed there at much greater length.

28. With reference to Lenin, Benjamin Schwartz could still write: "the a priori belief in the organic connection between the Communist Party and the proletariat lies at the very heart of the faith. The faith does, however, require certain visible signs. However little the party may heed the will of the actual proletarians, the existence of an industrial proletariat, however small, and the existence of some actual relationship between the proletariat, or part of the proletariat, and the party are considered essential to the party's continued existence." Benjamin I. Schwartz, *Chinese Communism and the Rise of Mao* (Cambridge, Mass.: Harvard University Press, 1951), 119.

29. "From what we know of his early years he seems to have become a Social-Democrat only after satisfying himself that the party, and the doctrine on which it was based, held out the only realistic hope for revolution in Russia. For Lenin, to be a Marxist meant to be a revolutionary." James E. Connor, "Preface," in James E. Connor, ed., *Lenin on Politics and Revolution* (New York: Pegasus, 1968), xviii.

30. "In Mao's case, . . . the impulse to revolution came before the commitment to Marxism as an intellectual system." Stuart A. Schram, *The Political Thought of Mao Tse-tung* (New York: Praeger, 1963), 17.

31. Karl Marx and Friedrich Engels, *The German Ideology. Parts I and III* (New York: International Publishers, 1947, 40.

32. Indeed, it has been argued "that there is a coherence of viewpoint and purpose throughout Lenin's theoretical writings, and that they do provide a clear guide to his intentions. Lenin's political thought had its focus in the problems of modernization of Russia." S. T. Glass, "The Single-Mindedness of Vladimir Ilich Ulyanov," *History of Political Thought* 8, no. 2 (Summer 1987): 277–87, at 277. This argument is supported with references to three dozen pieces of writing by Lenin, from his early "On the So-Called Market Question" (1893) to his last essay, "Better Fewer, but Better" (1923).

33. See, notably, "The Agrarian Programme of Social-Democracy in the First Russian Revolution, 1905–1907" (1908), in V. I. Lenin, *Collected Works* (Moscow: Progress Publishers, 1960–70), XIII, esp. 239–40, 296, 321–22, 346–54, 423. Lenin's *Collected Works* will henceforth be cited as *CW*.

34. "*We*, the workers, shall organise large-scale production on the basis of what capitalism has already created, relying on our own experience as workers, establishing strict, iron discipline backed up by the state power of the armed workers." "The State and Revolution" (1917), *CW*, XXV, 431. (Words in italics in this and in all subsequent quotations from Lenin appear in italics in the original.) Lichtheim refers to the Stalinist "idea of a social order created by force [as] perhaps the most 'un-Marxian' notion ever excogitated by professed Marxists." George Lichtheim, *Marxism. An Historical and Critical Study* (New York: Praeger, 1961), 370.

35. "Capitalist culture has *created* large-scale production, factories, railways, the postal service, telephones, etc., and *on this basis* the great majority of the functions of the old 'state power' has become so simplified and can be reduced to such exceedingly simple operations of registration, filing and checking that they can be easily performed by every literate person." "The State and Revolution" (1917), *CW*, XXV, 425–26. "It is quite possible, after the overthrow of the capitalists and the bureaucrats, to proceed immediately, overnight, to replace them in the *control* over production and distribution, in the work of *keeping account* of labour and products, by the armed workers, by the whole of the armed population. . . . The accounting and control necessary for this have been *simplified* by capitalism to the utmost and reduced to the extraordinarily simple operations—which any literate person can perform—of supervising and recording, knowledge of the four rules of arithmetic, and issuing appropriate receipts." Ibid., 478. See also "The Impending Catastrophe and How to Combat It" (1917), ibid., 323–69. Both this pamphlet and "The State and Revolution" were written by Lenin a few weeks before the Bolshevik seizure of power.

36. "Report of the Work of the Council of People's Commissars" (to the Eighth All-Russian Congress of Soviets, December 22, 1920), *CW*, XXXI, 516.

37. "Better Fewer, But Better" (1923), *CW*, XXXIII, 501.

38. At the Fourteenth Congress of the Communist Party of the Soviet Union (CPSU) in 1925, Stalin said: "The conversion of our country from an agrarian into an industrial country able to produce the machinery it needs by its own efforts—that is the essence, the basis of our general line." And later he commented on his statement of 1925: "The industrialization of the country would insure its economic independence, strengthen its power of defence and create the conditions for the victory of Socialism in the USSR." *History of the Communist Party of the Soviet Union (Bolsheviks). Short Course* (New York: International Publishers, 1939), 276.

39. "Address to the Second All-Russia Congress of Communist Organisations of the Peoples of the East" (1919), *CW*, XXX, 151.

40. "Better Fewer, But Better" (1923), *CW*, XXXIII, 500. Lenin defines the "East" as "India, China, etc." (ibid., 499), but then says that "in the last analysis, the outcome of the struggle will be determined by the fact that Russia, India, China, etc., account for the overwhelming majority of the population of the globe" (ibid., 500). He thus associates Russia with the "East."

41. I discuss Lenin's view of intellectuals as a response to his political needs in underdeveloped Russia in my essay "Lenin and Kautsky on the Role of Intellectuals in the Labor Movement: Different Conceptions in Different Environments," in my *Karl Kautsky: Marxism, Revolution, and Democracy* (New Brunswick, N.J.: Transaction Publishers, 1993). It was in order to elaborate the conclusions I reached in that article that I wrote the present book.

42. "What Is to Be Done?" (1902), *CW*, V, 375, 384–85. See also ibid., 426, 437, 475.

43. "The Urgent Tasks of Our Movement" (1900), *CW*, IV, 368.

44. "The Aim of the Proletarian Struggle in Our Revolution" (1909), *CW*, XV, 362–63.

45. See "The Workers' Party and the Peasantry" (1901), *CW*, IV, 420–28;

"The Agrarian Programme of Russian Social-Democracy" (1902), *CW*, VI, 105–48, esp. 146–47.

46. "Two Tactics of Social-Democracy in the Democratic Revolution" (1905), *CW*, IX, 17, 98, 100.

47. "Sketch of a Provisional Revolutionary Government" (1905), *CW*, VIII, 536.

48. "Two Tactics of Social-Democracy" (1905), *CW*, IX, 28–29, 48.

49. Ibid., 99.

50. Ibid., 98.

51. Ibid., 60. Lenin frequently emphasized the need for a "revolutionary-democratic dictatorship of the proletariat and the peasantry" in this period, for instance, ibid., 56, 84, 112, 128–29; "The Revolutionary-Democratic Dictatorship of the Proletariat and the Peasantry" (1905), *CW*, VIII, 293–303; "The Proletariat and Its Ally in the Russian Revolution" (1906), *CW*, XI, 374; "The Agrarian Programme of Social-Democracy in the First Russian Revolution (1908), *CW*, XIII, 353; "The Aim of the Proletarian Struggle in Our Revolution" (1909), *CW*, XV, 360–79.

52. "The Agrarian Programme of Social-Democracy in the First Russian Revolution" (1908), *CW*, XIII, 353; see also ibid., 349.

53. Ibid., 351.

54. Ibid., 421.

55. "Social-Democracy's Attitude Towards the Peasant Movement" (1905), *CW*, IX, 236–37.

56. Just before leaving Switzerland for Russia in April 1917, Lenin still wrote: "We know perfectly well that the proletariat of Russia is less organised, less prepared and less class-conscious than the proletariat of other countries. . . . Russia is a peasant country, one of the most backward of European countries. Socialism *cannot* triumph there *directly* and *immediately*. But the peasant character of the country, the vast reserve of land in the hands of the nobility, *may*, to judge from the experience of 1905, give tremendous sweep to the bourgeois-democratic revolution in Russia, and *may* make our revolution the *prologue* to the world socialist revolution, a *step* toward it." "Farewell Letter to the Swiss Workers" (1917), *CW*, XXIII, 371.

57. "Address to the Second All-Russia Congress of Communist Organisations of the Peoples of the East" (1919), *CW*, XXX, 160–61. In March 1919, Lenin wrote: "In October 1917 we seized power *together with the peasants as a whole*. This was a bourgeois revolution, inasmuch as the class struggle in the rural districts had not yet developed." "Eighth Congress of the R.C.P.(B.)" (1919), *CW*, XXIX, 203.

58. In his *The Class Struggles in France, 1848–1850*, Marx thus characterized the French peasants' vote for Louis Napoleon in 1848: "The symbol that expressed their entry into the revolutionary movement, clumsy but cunning, rascally but naive, oafish but sublime, a calculated superstition, a pathetic burlesque, an inspired but stupid anachronism, a momentous, historic piece of buffoonery, an undecipherable hieroglyph for the understanding of the civilized—this symbol bore unmistakably the physiognomy of the class which represents barbarism within civilization." Karl Marx, *Surveys from Exile* (New York: Vintage Books, 1974), 72.

59. While Marx and Engels could not regard the peasantry as an ally of the proletariat in the coming socialist revolution, they saw it as the "natural ally"

of the bourgeoisie in its revolutions against the aristocracy. They said so in strikingly similar language: Marx, with the revolutions of 1789 and 1848 in mind, in an article in *Die Neue Rheinische Zeitung*, July 30, 1848, in Karl Marx und Friedrich Engels, *Werke*, V (Berlin: Dietz Verlag, 1959), 283; and Engels, referring to the revolutions of 1525 and 1848, in "The Peasant War in Germany," in Friedrich Engels, *The German Revolutions* (Chicago: University of Chicago Press, 1967), 118. See also Engels' introduction to the first English edition (1892) of his *Socialism, Utopian and Scientific* (New York: International Publishers, 1935), 18, on the crucial role of the peasantry in the bourgeois risings of the German Reformation and the English and French Revolutions.

Karl Kautsky, who played a key role in blocking an SPD appeal to the peasantry—see Ingrid Gilcher-Holtey, *Das Mandat des Intellektuellen. Karl Kautsky und die Sozialdemokratie* (Berlin: Siedler Verlag, 1986), 103–18—saw the Russian peasantry as an ally of the proletariat in its revolution against tsarist autocracy, but not in a socialist revolution. See his "Triebkräfte und Aussichten der russischen Revolution," *Die Neue Zeit* 25/1 (1906): esp. 332. Lenin, in his preface (1907) to the Russian translation of this article, *CW*, XI, 408–13, enthusiastically used Kautsky's views to legitimate his own and to attack Plekhanov and the Mensheviks. See also Lenin's "The Proletariat and Its Ally in the Russian Revolution" (1906), *CW*, XI, 365–75; "The Agrarian Programme of Social-Democracy in the First Russian Revolution" (1908), *CW*, XIII, 353–54 (where Lenin calls the publication of Kautsky's article Bolshevism's "greatest *ideological* victory in international Social-Democracy"); and "The Aim of the Proletarian Struggle in Our Revolution" (1909), *CW*, XV, 375–77.

60. George Lichtheim, in his classic work *Marxism*, says "the uniqueness of Lenin—and of the Bolshevik organization which he founded and held together—lay in the decision to make the agrarian upheaval do the work of the proletarian revolution. . . . Throughout his career . . . he conveys a sense of determination to put a radical solution of the agrarian problem foremost among the tasks of the revolution. This was more than ordinary tactical realism; it reflected an order of priorities—ultimately a hierarchy of values—different from that of the average city-bred radical." Unlike me, Lichtheim holds that Lenin's central concern with "the agrarian problem . . . did not make him less of a Marxist, but it gave an emphasis to his cast of mind, which, to say the least, was unusual among Social-Democrats." Lichtheim, *Marxism*, 333–34.

Lichtheim also refers to Trotsky as writing that Lenin "staked everything on a radical solution of the peasant problem—to the extent of virtually identifying the 'bourgeois revolution' with the agrarian revolution." Ibid., 344. The reference is to Trotsky's introduction to the first Russian edition of his *The Permanent Revolution*, published in Berlin in 1930, where he says: "For Lenin, the liberation of the productive forces of bourgeois society from the fetters of serfdom signified, first and foremost, a radical solution of the agrarian question in the sense of complete liquidation of the landowning class and revolutionary redistribution of landownership." Leon Trotsky, *The Permanent Revolution* and *Results and Prospects* (New York: Merit Publishers, 1969), 127; see also Trotsky's *The Permanent Revolution* (New York: Pioneer Publishers, 1931), xxviii.

In a later essay, Lichtheim says that the replacement of the industrial proletariat by the peasantry as the revolutionary class "represents a complete break with Marxism, a circumstance that has not prevented some of its defenders from claiming the inheritance of Marx on the grounds that revolutionaries must always side with the exploited, whether they be slaves, serfs, or peasant proprietors victimized by colonial relationships. Admirable in its resolute disregard of all but moral considerations, this doctrine seems closer in spirit to Tolstoy or Gandhi than to the founders of modern socialism." While I regard this "complete break with Marxism" as Lenin's, Lichtheim sees it "as a consequence of the Maoist retreat from Marxism-Leninism." George Lichtheim, *Imperialism* (New York: Praeger, 1971), 104–05.

61. Alfred Meyer comments: "All of Lenin's pragmatism, all his readiness to try methods previously scored by the Marxist movement, all his contempt of the Menshevik preoccupation with accepted means and traditions of the workers' movement . . . [h]is elitism and his shifting attitude toward the various classes, his attitude toward national movements . . . every one of these formulas and devices, which arose as *ad hoc* changes in Marxist orthodoxy and could at first be justified only by the needs of the moment and the peculiarities of the Russian conditions . . . could be justified by the law of combined development, which converts the experience of western Europe, hitherto considered the standard pattern of development, into nothing but a unique, perhaps even a marginal one. Specifically, it becomes clear in the light of this hypothesis why the leaders of a revolutionary party in a backward country could adopt and develop the most radical ideology that had originated in an advanced society, why, in short, backward nations could become carriers of 'proletarian class consciousness.' " Alfred G. Meyer, *Leninism* (New York: Praeger, 1962), 268–69.

62. Franz Borkenau noted this briefly already in 1939, when he wrote: "Lenin's revolution is essentially not a proletarian revolution, it is '*the* revolution' of the intelligentsia, of the professional revolutionaries, but with the proletariat as their chief ally. Allies, however, are exchangeable. The course of the Russian dictatorship has proved that instead of the proletariat other groups could step in." Franz Borkenau, *World Communism. A History of the Communist International* (Ann Arbor: University of Michigan Press, 1962), 44.

63. Meyer notes that for Lenin "after 1905, the very word 'proletariat' gradually acquired a broader meaning, to include all those who sell their labor power to capitalists, including not only rural labor but even the intellectual proletariat. At the same time, the term 'proletariat' was more and more neglected; in its stead Lenin began to speak of the masses, the poor, the have-nots, or the toilers. . . . Both in Russia and elsewhere, Leninism after 1905 became a movement which based its strategy on the broad masses of the population, deserving the name 'proletariat' only in a wide sense, because they were composed more of peasants than of workers." Meyer, *Leninism*, 127–28.

64. Marx objected even to the term "the working people" (*das arbeitende Volk*) in the Gotha Program, when he wrote: "The majority of the 'toiling people' in Germany consists of peasants and not of proletarians." Karl Marx, *Critique of the Gotha Program* (New York: International Publishers, 1938), 16.

65. "Letter from Afar" (1917), *CW*, XXIII, 304.

66. "What Is to Be Done" (1902), *CW*, V, 428.

67. Ibid., 422, 429.

68. Ibid., 430, 431. "The more we *confine* the membership of such an organization to people who are professionally engaged in revolutionary activity . . . the *greater* will be the number of people from the working class *and from the other social classes* who will be able to join the movement and perform active work in it." Ibid., p. 464; last italics added.

69. Speaking of "the Russian Communists' practical activities in the former tsarist colonies, in such backward countries as Turkestan," Lenin—very clearly indicating that the "we" he had in mind are not workers—says: "There is practically no industrial proletariat in these countries. Nevertheless, we have assumed, we must assume, the role of leader even there. . . . The practical results of our work have . . . shown that . . . we are in a position to inspire in the masses an urge for independent political thinking and independent political action, even where a proletariat is practically non-existent. . . . The idea of Soviet organization is a simple one, and is applicable, not only to proletarian, but also to peasant feudal and semi-feudal relations." "Report of the Commission on the National and the Colonial Questions" (1920), *CW*, XXXI, 242–43. "The ideas and principles of Soviet government are understood and immediately applicable, not only in the industrially developed countries, not only in those which have a social basis like the proletariat, but also in those which have the peasantry as their basis." "Report on the Work of the Council of People's Commissars" (to the Eighth All-Russia Congress of Soviets) (1920), *CW*, XXXI, 490. See also Lenin's earlier "Address to the Second All-Russia Congress of Communist Organisations of the Peoples of the East" (1919), *CW*, XXX, 151–62.

70. "Report on the International Situation and the Fundamental Tasks of the Communist International" (1920), *CW*, XXXI, 232.

71. Ibid.

72. "Preliminary Draft Theses on the National and the Colonial Questions" (1920), *CW*, XXXI, 146, 148.

73. "Report on the International Situation and the Fundamental Tasks of the Communist International" (1920), *CW*, XXXI, 232.

74. "Report of the Commission on the National and the Colonial Questions" (1920), *CW*, XXXI, 243.

75. "Preliminary Draft Theses on the National and the Colonial Questions" (1920), *CW*, XXXI, 146.

76. Ibid., 149.

77. Ibid., 149, 150. In November 1919, Lenin had advised Communists whom he described as representing " . . . the peoples of the East[:] . . . You will have to base yourselves on the bourgeois nationalism which is awakening, and must awaken, among those peoples, and which has its historical justification." "Address to the Second All-Russia Congress of Communist Organisations of the Peoples of the East" (1919), *CW*, XXX, 162.

78. "Report of the Commission on the National and the Colonial Questions" (1920), *CW*, XXXI, 241.

79. In 1919, he said to "Communist comrades representing [Communist] Moslem organisations of the East": " . . . the majority of the Eastern peoples are typical representatives of the working people—not workers who have passed through the school of capitalist factories, but typical representatives of the working and exploited peasant masses who are victims of medieval oppression. . . . You must be able to apply that theory and practice [of communism] to conditions

in which the bulk of the population are peasants, and in which the task is to wage a struggle against medieval survivals and not against capitalism." "Address to the Second All-Russia Congress of Communist Organisations of the Peoples of the East" (1919), *CW*, XXX, 151, 161.

80. "Preliminary Draft Theses on the National and the Colonial Questions" (1920), *CW*, XXXI, 149, 148.

81. "Report of the Commission on the National and the Colonial Questions" (1920), *CW*, XXXI, 242.

82. "Lenin was not a philosopher or social theorist of even secondary importance. To think otherwise is quite to mistake the nature of his genius. His more theoretical works, had anyone else written them, would now be read by no one." Plamenatz, *German Marxism*, 221.

83. See the explanation offered in a discussion in the Soviet Academy of Sciences of why Mongolia could have a proletarian government even though, admittedly, there was no proletariat in Mongolia. "Discussion of the Character and Effect of People's Democracy in the Orient," translated in *Current Digest of the Soviet Press* 4, no. 20 (June 28, 1952): 5, 7.

As John Plamenatz wrote very bluntly at about the time of this discussion, "If the 'party of the proletariat' can make a 'proletarian' revolution without greatly caring what the workers think, if it can know what is good for them better than they know it themselves, . . . why should it not act on their behalf even before there are enough of them to constitute an important class in society? . . . The later Communists have improved on Lenin. They have formed parties of the proletariat where no proletariat exists; they have done it in China and Yugoslavia. The members of those parties are nearly all intellectuals or peasants, but their avowed purpose is to establish a proletarian state. They first make a revolution and then set about creating the industries without which, according to Marx, no proletarian state can exist. They first capture the 'superstructure' and then use it to transform the 'foundation'—so that 'proletarian revolution,' from being an effect of mature industrialism, becomes a prelude to it." Plamenatz, *German Marxism*, 238.

Plamenatz also said of Lenin that "he saw, more clearly than any other Marxist, that a band of revolutionaries might, in a backward country already deeply affected by industrialism and western ideas, exploit the ambitions, hatreds and fears of all classes and political groups to so good effect as to be able to take power in the name of the proletariat; and he found it possible to persuade himself and others that this seizure of power would be a proletarian revolution." Ibid., 221.

84. Karl Marx, "Preface" to *A Contribution to the Critique of Political Economy*, in Karl Marx, *Early Writings* (New York: Vintage Books, 1975), 425. I have slightly corrected the translation.

85. The Erfurt Program and a number of earlier drafts are reprinted in an appendix to Gilcher-Holtey, *Das Mandat*, 332–51. I am not suggesting that Marxist determinists, like Marx and Kautsky, held the nonsensical view often ascribed to them, especially to Kautsky, that history is some kind of force that proceeds independently of the will and actions of men. It was Marx who wrote "Men make their own history"; he added, however, "but they do not make it just as they please; they do not make it under circumstances chosen by themselves,

but under circumstances directly found, given and transmitted from the past."
Karl Marx, *The Eighteenth Brumaire of Louis Bonaparte* (New York: International
Publishers, n.d.), 13. In an earlier work, Marx and Engels had written: "*History*
does *nothing*, it 'does *not* possess immense wealth,' it 'fights *no* battles'! It is,
rather, *man*, real, living man who does all this, who possesses and fights; it is
not 'history' that uses man as a means to pursue *its* goals—as if it were an
individual person—but it is *nothing* but the activity of man pursuing his goals."
Friedrich Engels and Karl Marx, "Die heilige Familie," in Karl Marx and Friedrich
Engels, *Werke*, II (Berlin: Dietz Verlag, 1962), 98.

Kautsky, in his commentary on the Erfurt Program, wrote: "When one speaks
of the irresistibility and natural necessity of social development, one obviously
presupposes that men are men and not dead puppets; men with certain needs
and passions, with certain physical and mental powers that they seek to use in
their own interest. . . . We consider the collapse of present-day society inevitable,
because we know that economic development produces, with natural necessity,
conditions that compel the exploited to fight against private property." *Das
Erfurter Programm* (19th ed.; Bonn: J. H. W. Dietz Nachf., 1974), 102.

86. Stuart R. Schram, "On the Quotations," in Mao Tse-tung, *Quotations from
Chairman Mao Tse-tung* (New York: Bantam Books, 1967), xi.

87. Translated in Jerome Ch'en, *Mao* (Englewood Cliffs, N.J.: Prentice-Hall,
1969), 113.

88. "Bankruptcy of the Idealist Conception of History" (September 16, 1969),
in Mao Tse-tung, *Selected Works* (New York: International Publishers, 1954–56),
V, 454. In November 1938, Mao had written: "Every Communist must grasp
the truth: 'Political power grows out of the barrel of a gun.' " "Problems of War
and Strategy," ibid., II, 272.

89. Martin Kenner and James Petras, eds., *Fidel Castro Speaks* (New York:
Grove Press, 1969), 278.

90. An interesting study of revolutionary development in Ethiopia points
out that Soviet ideologists could justify a socialist revolution in that country "by
arguing that Lenin himself came out categorically against overemphasis on tech-
nical-economic prerequisites as well as against rigid, deterministic political preconditions for socialist revolution." Edmond J. Keller, *Revolutionary Ethiopia*
(Bloomington: Indiana University Press, 1988), 197–98.

A historian of Cambodia states that the Communist leadership's choice "to
wage revolution everywhere in Cambodia did not spring from a study of Cambodian social conditions . . . but from a conviction . . . that a recognizably Communist revolution needed to be waged. If the right preconditions did not exist,
that problem could be overcome by revolutionary fervor. The absence of a proletariat in Cambodia, for example, was not seen as an impediment to progress."
David P. Chandler, *The Tragedy of Cambodian History* (New Haven: Yale University
Press, 1991), 239. In a footnote, ibid., 364, he quotes Kathleen Gough, "Roots
of the Pol Pot Regime in Kampuchea," in Leland Donald, ed., *Themes in Ethnology
and Culture History* (Meerut, India: Archana Publications, 1987), 139–41, listing
as one of the bases of Cambodian Communist ideology Maoism's "utopian and
idealist disregard of material and objective conditions; an apocalyptic voluntarism."

91. As Stuart Schram put it: "If Lenin arbitrarily identified the Communist

Party with the true will of the real proletariat, Mao and his friends affirmed that the Party can substitute itself for a virtually nonexistent proletariat as the leader of the agrarian revolution." Schram, *The Political Thought of Mao Tse-tung*, 78.

Benjamin Schwartz wrote in 1951: "Chinese Communism in its Maoist development demonstrates in fact that a communist party organized along Leninist lines and imbued with a sincere faith in certain basic Marxist-Leninist tenets can exist quite apart from any organic connection with the proletariat. The experience of Chinese Communism thus casts a doubt on the whole organic conception of the relation of party to class." Schwartz, *Chinese Communism*, 191.

Commenting on this last sentence, Stuart Schram wrote in 1963: "This is the basic question raised not only by Mao's thought, but by that of Lenin and by the whole history of Communism for the past half century. It is incontestable that, as Schwartz has put it, Mao has marched through doors that Lenin only opened. Whether Mao, in carrying one step further the divorce between Party and class initiated by Lenin in *What Is To Be Done?*, has contributed to the 'decomposition' of Marxism, or whether he is merely enabling it better to exploit the reactions of protest in agrarian societies exposed to the impact of industrialization, is another question." Schram, *The Political Thought of Mao Tse-tung*, 36–37.

92. "Report of an Investigation into the Peasant Movement in Hunan" (1927), Mao, *Selected Works*, I, 32. For the 1951 edition of his works, Mao amended passages in this 1927 report, which suggest that poor peasants take the initiative in the revolution, by adding: "They accept the leadership of the Communist Party most willingly."

Schram, stressing the voluntarist character of Leninism, comments on the Hunan Report: "It is essentially a-Marxist. But at the same time it reveals vividly Mao's 'natural Leninism,' which . . . manifests itself . . . in the firm grasp of the principle that political struggle is the key to economic struggle. The proposition that politics always takes priority over economics in periods of revolution is in fact the very heart of Leninism." Schram, *The Political Thought of Mao Tse-tung*, 33.

93. The use of the term "propertyless class" in Chinese to render the Marxian word "proletariat" also obscures the difference between industrial workers and landless peasants.

94. See Mao Tse-tung, "The Chinese Revolution and the Chinese Communist Party" (1939), *Selected Works*, III, 72–101, esp. 88–92, 97; "On New Democracy" (1940), ibid., 106–56, esp. 150. See also "On the People's Democratic Dictatorship" (1949), ibid., V, 411–24, esp. 415, 417, 421. Strikingly pro-capitalist statements appear in Mao Tse-tung, "On Coalition Government" (1945), ibid., IV, 244–315, esp. 273–78, 299.

95. Once in power, the Chinese Communists did seek the help of capitalists as experts on industrialization. Liu Shao-chi, then the leading Party theorist after Mao, is reported to have addressed Chinese businessmen along the following lines: "As Communists, we consider that you are exploiting your workers; but we realize that, at the present stage of China's economic development, such exploitation is unavoidable and even socially useful. What we want is for you to go ahead and develop production as fast as possible and we will do what we can to help." Quoted by Michael Lindsay in Otto B. van der Sprenkel, ed., *New*

China: Three Views (New York: John Day, 1951), 139. For more of this statement and two others conveying the same message, see my *Communism and the Politics of Development*, 46.

96. Deprived of its Marxian meaning, the term "class struggle" has been retained by the Chinese Communists to refer to their conflicts with opposing or dissident elements.

97. Thus, "feudal" elements can be added to "bourgeois" ones, as when Mao lists "the allies that should be won over (middle peasants, small independent craftsmen and traders, the middle bourgeoisie, students, teachers, professors and ordinary intellectuals, ordinary government employees, professionals *and enlightened gentry*)." "On Some Important Problems of the Party's Present Policy" (1948), Mao, *Selected Works*, V, 181–82; italics added. "The motive forces of the Viet-Nam revolution at present are the people comprising primarily the workers, peasants, petty-bourgeoisie and national bourgeoisie, followed by the patriotic and progressive personages and landlords." "Platform of the Viet-Nam Lao Dong Party," *People's China* 3, no. 9 (May 1, 1951): supp.

98. "Speech by Liu Shao-chi at the Conference of Trade Unions of Asia and Oceania," *For a Lasting Peace, for a People's Democracy*, December 30, 1949, 2. Also in *Pravda*, January 4, 1950; translated in *Soviet Press Translations*, 5, no. 6 (March 15, 1950): 168–72.

99. With respect to the Indian Communist Party, I documented it fully in my *Moscow and the Communist Party of India* (New York: John Wiley, 1956; reprint, Westport, CT: Greenwood Press, 1982).

100. I did so in the 1950s and 1960s in a dozen writings collected in my *Communism and the Politics of Development*.

101. These statements, along with similar ones by a number of Soviet writers, are quoted, respectively, from TASS International News Report, May 24, 1964, and from *Pravda* and *Izvestia* of December 22, 1963, in Uri Ra'anan, "Moscow and the 'Third World'," *Problems of Communism* 14, no. 1 (January–February 1965): 24, 27; Ra'anan also stresses opposition within both the Soviet and the Arab Communist parties to this friendly approach to non-Leninist modernizing regimes in underdeveloped countries. Also in 1964, Khrushchev awarded the Algerian leader Ben Bella and Nasser the title Hero of the Soviet Union, though the Egyptian Communists had just been released from jail and their Party remained illegal.

102. Writing in the period between Castro's victory on New Year's Day 1959 and his declaration that he was a "Marxist-Leninist," the general secretary of the Cuban Popular Socialist Party (the Communist Party), with its principal strength in Havana, stated clearly that the Cuban Revolution had been non-Communist: "The armed struggle was initiated by the petty bourgeoisie. The working-class action could not be the decisive factor of the revolution. . . . The revolution marched triumphantly from the countryside to the towns, from the provinces to the capital. The political leadership of the armed struggle was in the hands of the petty bourgeoisie while the rebel army consisted mainly of poor peasants and farm laborers." Blas Roca, "The Cuban Revolution in Action," *World Marxist Review* 2, no. 8 (August 1959): 18.

103. For documentation of the developments mentioned in this and the pre-

ceding paragraph, see my *Communism and the Politics of Development*, 97–100, 109–13, 146, 148–51, 154.

104. "Preliminary Draft Theses on the National and the Colonial Questions" (1920), *CW*, XXXI, 150. During the 1905 Revolution in Russia, when the issue of cooperation with the bourgeoisie also arose, Lenin had written: "A Social-Democrat must never for a moment forget that the proletariat will inevitably have to wage a class struggle for socialism even against the most democratic and republican bourgeoisie and petty bourgeoisie. This is beyond doubt. Hence, the absolute necessity of a separate, independent, strictly class party of Social-Democracy." "Two Tactics of Social-Democracy in the Democratic Revolution" (1905), *CW*, IX, 85.

105. On August 10, 1990, the *New York Times* quoted two Nicaraguan Sandinista leaders as saying that the Soviet Union was "no longer a sufficient guide for orienting the political activity of the Sandinista Front" and "if we think the contradiction in this country is between the proletariat and the bourgeoisie, we will have the wrong approach."

106. In April 1990, the ruling Communist party in Mongolia, the Mongolian People's Revolutionary Party, dropped the word "Communism" from its constitution but, according to a Party spokesman, "remains Marxist-Leninist." *New York Times*, April 13, 1990, A4. In 1991, it governed in coalition with other parties and itself split, but in June 1992 it won an overwhelming victory in supposedly free parliamentary elections. The Albanian Communist Party of Labor remained strong enough to win an election in 1991, but, now renamed the Socialist Party, shared power for some time with a non-Communist opposition and then lost a parliamentary election and the presidency in 1992.

107. The governments of Angola, Mozambique, Benin, and the Congo renounced Marxism-Leninism, and Marxist-Leninist Southern Yemen merged with non–Marxist-Leninist Yemen.

108. In March 1990, Mengistu had changed the name of his Ethiopian Workers Party to the Democratic Unity Party of Ethiopia, and a billboard of Marx, Engels, and Lenin in Revolution Square in Addis Ababa had been removed. The statue of Lenin in Addis Ababa was torn down as the Mengistu regime fell. Its successors (see note 1), now desirous of U.S. support, have discovered their attachment to "democracy" and "free enterprise." The new leader in Addis Ababa, Meles Zenawi, a former medical student who led the Marxist-Leninist League of Tigre, had once favored an "Albanian-style hard-line Communist system" (*New York Times*, May 29, 1991, A4), but "it seems doubtful that the hard-line Marxist talk, prevalent during the guerrilla war, will stick when it comes to the reality of governing." "Much of the Marxist rhetoric of the new rulers in Addis Ababa derives from their long years in the bush, when rote learning from Marxist tracts was part of the training." Jane Perlez, "A New Chance for a Fractured Land," *New York Times Magazine*, September 22, 1991, 51.

109. The *New York Times* of December 9, 1991, reported on two Communist party congresses. The South African Communist Party, significant because of its close links with some of the leadership of the African National Congress, proclaimed its "Marxism-Leninism" and its identification with Cuba. The Communist Party of the United States, with 3,000 dues-paying members, denounced

the Soviet leadership of Gorbachev and Yeltsin as well as factionalism within the Party. One dissident said, "We don't want to air our dirty Lenin in public."

110. Lenin quotes "the Menshevik Maslov" as saying "a dictatorship of the proletariat and the peasantry would run counter to the whole course of economic development"; he responds: "It is precisely here that the roots of the divergencies between Bolshevism and Menshevism must be sought." He then adds: "The struggle between Bolshevism and Menshevism is . . . a struggle over the question whether to . . . overthrow the hegemony of the liberals over the peasantry." "The Historical Meaning of the Inner-Party Struggle in Russia" (1910), CW, XVI, 376, 378.

111. I outlined this track of "modernization from without" and contrasted it to the one of "modernization from within" in my *The Political Consequences of Modernization*.

112. While the profound differences between the Marxist Mensheviks and the Leninist Bolsheviks were long obscured by questions of personalities and of formal party structure, it is interesting to note that the Menshevik Pavel Axelrod, as early as 1903, when the split in the Russian Social-Democratic Party occurred, saw the conflict as one between the "subjective aims" of Marxists and the "objective reality" of their Party as it had responded to Russian conditions. In an article in *Iskra* no. 55 (December 15, 1903) and no. 57 (January 15, 1904), as summarized and quoted in Abraham Ascher, "Axelrod and Kautsky," *Slavic Review* 26, no. 1 (March 1967): 97, Axelrod wrote: "Subjectively, Marxists were committed to promoting the 'class consciousness and political initiative of the laboring masses' and to uniting them into an 'independent revolutionary force under the banner of Social Democracy.' They favored a political movement in which the masses would participate actively and exercise control. In fact, however, a highly centralized party had evolved because of the conditions of secrecy and oppression under which Marxists had to operate in Russia. The enormous success of this type of organization had infected the leadership with a 'fetishism of centralism,' or belief that the party should be controlled by a small group of revolutionaries—the very antithesis of the Marxist ideal."

113. I developed this argument at some length in my "Myth, Self-Fulfilling Prophecy and Symbolic Reassurance in the East-West Conflict," *Journal of Conflict Resolution* 9, no. 1 (March 1965): 1–17, reprinted in my *Communism and the Politics of Development*, 121–44.

114. I draw parallels between the history of the PCF and PCI, on the one hand, and that of the SPD, on the other, in my article "Karl Kautsky and Eurocommunism," *Studies in Comparative Communism* 14, no. 1 (Spring 1981): 3–44, reprinted in my *Karl Kautsky: Marxism, Revolution, and Democracy*.

115. Maurice Zeitlin and Richard Earl Ratcliff, "Research Methods for the Analysis of the Internal Structure of Dominant Classes: The Case of Landlords and Capitalists in Chile," *Latin American Research Review* 10, no. 3 (Fall 1975): 5–61.

116. As quoted from *El Siglo* (Santiago), December 2, 1970, in William E. Ratliff, *Castroism and Communism in Latin America, 1959–1976* (Washington, D.C.: American Enterprise Institute, 1976), 162–63, Luis Corvalán, the secretary-general of the Chilean Communist Party, said of the program of the Popular Unity coalition that it was meant to "liberate Chile from imperialist domination, to

destroy the power centers of the oligarchy, to take the country out of under-development, to build an independent and modern economy, to create a new condition of justice and a more advanced democracy, and to begin the construc-tion of socialism." Some of these points are clearly Leninist, while those about the "oligarchy," "justice" and "democracy," and "socialism" can, given the ambiguity of these terms, be seen as either Marxist or Leninist.

117. "La rivoluzione contro il *'Capitale,'* " *Avanti*, November 24, 1917, in An-tonio Gramsci, *Scritti giovanili* (Turin: Einaudi, 1958), 150. Between the two passages quoted, giving evidence both of Benedetto Croce's influence on him and of the voluntarism typical of modernizing intellectuals in underdeveloped countries, Gramsci says that the Bolsheviks "deny some assertions of *Capital"* but that they live "Marxist thought, which does not die, which is the continuation of Italian and German idealist thought and which in Marx had become contam-inated by positivistic and naturalistic incrustations. And this thought always puts as the most important factor of history not brute economic facts, but man, the societies of men [who develop] a collective social will and comprehend economic facts and judge them and adapt them to their will."

118. "Gramsci had intuitively grasped the nature of Leninism, as the theory and practice of a revolution in a retarded country where the masses were sud-denly hurled upon the political stage under the leadership of the Bolshevik vanguard." Lichtheim, *Marxism*, 369.

119. In a footnote to a thoughtful essay reviewing the literature on the history of the German Social-Democratic Party, Geoff Eley says: "Unfortunately most work on Luxemburg, Kautsky and other representatives of the SPD's Marxist tradition has been preoccupied with defining their relationship to post–1917 Leninism, not the most auspicious of beginnings for a well-contextualized his-torical understanding . . . locating particular theoreticians in the specific historical circumstances that lent coherence to their ideas. But this (an elementary principle for any materialist sociology of knowledge, one might have thought) is all too frequently absent from Marxist discussions of their own tradition." "Joining Two Histories: The SPD and the German Working Class, 1860–1914," in Eley's *From Unification to Nazism* (Boston: Allen and Unwin, 1986), 195, n. 27.

120. Paul Hollander, who denounces such intellectuals, has even discovered a few admirers of Enver Hoxha's Albania and Samora Machel's Mozambique. Paul Hollander, *Political Pilgrims. Travels of Western Intellectuals to the Soviet Union, China, and Cuba, 1928–1978* (New York: Oxford University Press, 1981), 275–77, 481–82.

121. In his preface to the first edition of *Capital*, Marx had written: "The country that is more developed industrially only shows, to the less developed, the image of its own future." It is impossible to conceive of Marx reversing this statement.

122. Even in the 1930s, when I attended the Gymnasium in Vienna, the only non-European country ever mentioned in eight years of history instruction was ancient Egypt.

123. The assumption that German Marxists would feel involved in Russian politics because Russia was European, in sharp contrast to their attitude toward more distant countries, is nicely, though not deliberately, illustrated by the opening sentence of an article on Russia by Alexander Helphand (Parvus), a

Marxist writer active in Germany and Russia. In it, he says he will deal with Russian political developments quite objectively, "as if it was not we ourselves who were involved but someone else, as if events there took place not in Russia, but in some distant land beyond mountains and oceans, in China or in Ethiopia or in the land of cannibals." Parvus, "Die gegenwärtige politische Lage Russlands und die Aussichten für die Zukunft," *Die Neue Zeit* 24/2 (1906): 108. Helphand-Parvus could not know that the Russian future he sought to predict would, in important respects, be less similar to the future of Germany than to that of China and Ethiopia, which in his mind were linked with "the land of cannibals," but where traditional empires were also to be overthrown by revolutionary modernizers.

124. I sought to demonstrate this in my book *The Politics of Aristocratic Empires* (Chapel Hill: University of North Carolina Press, 1982).

125. Similarities and differences being in the eye of the beholder and a matter of emphasis, this is not to suggest that parallels between the Russian and the French revolutions cannot be valid and useful for certain kinds of analyses. There is a long tradition of work comparing the two revolutions, from Crane Brinton, *The Anatomy of Revolution* (New York: W. W. Norton, 1938; rev. ed., New York: Vintage Books, 1965) to Theda Skocpol, *States and Social Revolutions* (New York: Cambridge University Press, 1979), to name only two insightful non-Marxist studies.

126. Trotsky's characterization of Stalin as "Thermidorian" figures prominently in his attack on Stalin, while Deutscher, who sympathized with Trotsky, stressed parallels between Stalin and Napoleon. Isaac Deutscher, "The French Revolution and the Russian Revolution. Some Suggestive Analogies," *World Politics* 4, no. 3 (April 1952): 369–81.

127. Five each on China (1886, 1900, 1908, 1911, 1912) and what was then called Persia (1892, two in 1910, two in 1911), four on Turkey (1900, 1902, 1904, 1908), three on India (1891, 1897, 1900), two each on Mexico (both in 1911) and on Egypt and the Sudan (1883, 1884), one each on Cameroon (1888) and on three colonies in Southeast Asia (1884, 1896, 1914).

128. "The War in China" (1900), *CW*, IV, 372–77.

129. "Inflammable Material in World Politics" (1908), *CW*, XV, 182–88; "Events in the Balkans and in Persia" (1908), *CW*, XV, 220–30.

130. "Democracy and Narodism in China" (1912), *CW*, XVIII, 163–69; "Regenerated China" (1912), *CW*, XVIII, 400–01. The following year, Lenin devoted a two-page article to "the revolutionary democratic movement" in the Dutch East Indies. "The Awakening of Asia" (1913), *CW*, XIX, 85–86.

131. "Democracy and Narodism in China" (1912), *CW*. XVIII, 165.

132. Ibid.

133. Michael Pawlowitsch, "Die revolutionäre Bewegung und die politischen Parteien im heutigen China," *Die Neue Zeit* 29/2 (1911): 37–42, 80–84; and "Die grosse chinesische Revolution," ibid., 30/1 (1911–12): 372–85, 494–506, 557–70. Twenty-five years earlier, Kautsky had predicted that railroads would "revolutionize the Chinese people." "Die chinesischen Eisenbahnen und das europäische Proletariat," ibid., 4 (1886): 515–25, 529–49, at 547.

134. Quoted in Tony Cliff, *Lenin* (London: Pluto Press, 1975), 78, from Z. Krzhizhanovskaia, *Neskolko shtrikov iz zhizhni Lenina* (Moscow, 1925), II, 49.

135. I cannot be absolutely certain that Lenin nowhere referred to Mexico, but neither the index to the 4th Russian edition of Lenin's *Collected Works* (Moscow: Government Publishing House of Political Literature, 1956) nor the index to works newly included in the full collection of the works of Lenin (Moscow: Government Publishing House of Political Literature, 1966) contains an entry "Mexico." The volumes of Lenin's English-language *Collected Works* from 1910 to 1924 contain no subject indexes (except XXXVIII, *Philosophical Notebooks*), but vols. XXXIV–XLV, consisting of letters, messages, speeches, draft resolutions, and notebooks, do have name indices. There is no reference in them to Porfirio Díaz, Francisco Madero, Francisco Villa, or Emiliano Zapata. I also checked, more haphazardly, the indices of other collections of Lenin's writings and of several dozen secondary works on Lenin without finding a single reference to Mexico. In 1921, Lenin did have a meeting with a Mexican Communist and an interview with an Argentine Communist with whom he discussed agrarian reform in Mexico. See articles in *Voprosy istorii* [Problems of History; Moscow] (1961): 1, 163–66, and (1984): 11, 84–92.

136. Paul Zierold, "Die Revolution in Mexiko," *Die Neue Zeit* 29/2 (1911): 396–402.

137. A quite unsystematic and incomplete survey of works by and about these authors revealed no reference to the Mexican Revolution. Trotsky, of course, spent his last years in exile in Mexico.

138. "The Discussion on Self-Determination Summed Up" (1916), CW, XXII, 357.

139. "Democracy and Narodism in China" (1912), CW, XVIII, 163–69.

140. "Our Revolution" (1923), CW, XXXIII, 477.

141. Ibid., 480.

Bibliography

Adler, Victor. *Aufsätze, Reden und Briefe.* Vienna: Wiener Volksbuchhandlung, 1929.

Agger, Ben. *Western Marxism. An Introduction.* Santa Monica, Calif.: Goodyear, 1979.

Allen, William Sheridan. *The Nazi Seizure of Power.* New York: New Viewpoints, 1973.

Anderson, Perry. *Considerations on Western Marxism.* London: NLB, 1976.

Ascher, Abraham. "Axelrod and Kautsky." *Slavic Review* 26, no. 1 (March 1967): 94–112.

Avinieri, Shlomo, ed. *Karl Marx on Colonialism and Modernization.* Garden City, N.Y.: Doubleday, 1968.

Bauer, Otto. "Einleitung." In Victor Adler, *Aufsätze, Reden und Briefe.*

Bernstein, Eduard. *Evolutionary Socialism.* New York: Schocken Books, 1961.

———. "Der Kampf der Sozialdemokratie und die Revolution der Gesellschaft." *Die Neue Zeit* 16/1 (1898): 484–97, 548–57.

Borkenau, Franz. *World Communism. A History of the Communist International.* Ann Arbor: University of Michigan Press, 1962.

Brailsford, H. N. "Introduction." In Julius Braunthal, *In Search of the Millennium.*

Braunthal, Julius. *In Search of the Millennium.* London: Gollancz, 1945.

Brinton, Crane. *The Anatomy of Revolution.* New York: W. W. Norton, 1938. Rev. ed., New York: Vintage Books, 1965.

Chandler, David P. *The Tragedy of Cambodian History.* New Haven: Yale University Press, 1991.

Ch'en, Jerome. *Mao.* Englewood Cliffs, N.J.: Prentice-Hall, 1969.

Cliff, Tony. *Lenin.* London: Pluto Press, 1975.

Connor, James E., ed. *Lenin on Politics and Revolution.* New York: Pegasus, 1968.

Deutscher, Isaac. "The French Revolution and the Russian Revolution. Some Suggestive Analogies." *World Politics* 4, no. 3 (April 1952): 369–81.

"Discussion of the Character and Effect of People's Democracy in the Orient." *Current Digest of the Soviet Press* 4, no. 20 (June 28, 1952): 3–7.

Eley, Geoff. *From Unification to Nazism*. Boston: Allen and Unwin, 1986.

Engels, Friedrich. *The German Revolutions*. Chicago: University of Chicago Press, 1967.

———. *Socialism, Utopian and Scientific*. New York: International Publishers, 1935.

Evans, Richard J., ed. *The German Working Class, 1888–1933*. London: Croom Helm, 1982.

Gilcher-Holtey, Ingrid. *Das Mandat des Intellektuellen. Karl Kautsky und die Sozialdemokratie*. Berlin: Siedler Verlag, 1986.

Glass, S. T. "The Single-Mindedness of Vladimir Ilich Ulyanov." *History of Political Thought* 8, no. 2 (Summer 1987): 277–87.

Gough, Kathleen. "Roots of the Pol Pot Regime in Kampuchea." In Leland Donald, ed., *Themes in Ethnology and Culture History*. Meerut, India: Archana Publications, 1987.

Gramsci, Antonio. *Scritti giovanili*. Turin: Einaudi, 1958.

Groh, Dieter. *Negative Integration und revolutionärer Attentismus. Die deutsche Sozialdemokratie am Vorabend des esten Weltkrieges*. Frankfurt am Main: Ullstein-Propyläen, 1973.

Guttsman, W. L. *The German Social Democratic Party, 1875–1933. From Ghetto to Government*. London: Allen and Unwin, 1981.

Hall, Alex. *Scandal, Sensation and Social Democracy*. Cambridge: Cambridge University Press, 1977.

Helphand, Alexander. *See* Parvus.

History of the Communist Party of the Soviet Union (Bolsheviks). Short Course. New York: International Publishers, 1939.

Hollander, Paul. *Political Pilgrims. Travels of Western Intellectuals to the Soviet Union, China, and Cuba, 1928–1978*. New York: Oxford University Press, 1981.

Jacoby, Russell. *Dialectic of Defeat: Contours of Western Marxism*. Cambridge: Cambridge University Press, 1981.

Jones, Gareth Stedman. *Western Marxism. A Critical Reader*. London: NLB, 1977.

Kautsky, John H. *Communism and the Politics of Development*. New York: John Wiley, 1968.

———. "Comparative Communism Versus Comparative Politics." *Studies in Comparative Communism* 6, nos. 1 and 2 (Spring/Summer 1973): 135–70.

———. "Karl Kautsky and Eurocommunism." *Studies in Comparative Communism* 14, no. 1 (Spring 1981): 3–44.

———. *Karl Kautsky: Marxism, Revolution, and Democracy*. New Brunswick, N.J.: Transaction Publishers, 1993.

———. *Moscow and the Communist Party of India*. New York: John Wiley, 1956; reprint, Westport, CT: Greenwood Press, 1982.

———. "Myth, Self-Fulfilling Prophecy and Symbolic Reassurance in the East-West Conflict." *Journal of Conflict Resolution* 9, no. 1 (March 1965): 1–17.

———. *Patterns of Modernizing Revolutions: Mexico and the Soviet Union*. Sage Professional Papers in Comparative Politics, 5. Beverly Hills, Calif.: Sage, 1975.

———. *The Political Consequences of Modernization*. New York: John Wiley, 1972; reprint, Huntington, NY: Krieger, 1980.

———. *The Politics of Aristocratic Empires*. Chapel Hill: University of North Carolina Press, 1982.

Kautsky, Karl. "Die chinesischen Einsenbahnen und das europäische Proletariat." *Die Neue Zeit* 4 (1886): 515–25, 529–49.

———. *Das Erfurter Programm*. 19th ed. Bonn: J.H.W. Dietz Nachf., 1974.

———. *The Materialist Conception of History*. Abridged edition. New Haven: Yale University Press, 1988.

———. "Die Revision des Programms der Sozialdemokratie in Oesterreich." *Die Neue Zeit* 20/1 (1901): 68–82.

———. "Triebkräfte und Aussichten der russischen Revolution." *Die Neue Zeit* 25/1 (1906): 324–33.

Keller, Edmond J. *Revolutionary Ethiopia*. Bloomington: Indiana University Press, 1988.

Kenner, Martin, and James Petras, eds. *Fidel Castro Speaks*. New York: Grove Press, 1969.

Lenin, V. I. *Collected Works*. 45 vols. Moscow: Progress Publishers, 1960–70.

Lichtheim, George. *Imperialism*. New York: Praeger, 1971.

———. *Marxism. An Historical and Critical Study*. New York: Praeger, 1961.

Lidtke, Vernon L. *The Alternative Culture. Socialist Labor in Imperial Germany*. New York: Oxford University Press, 1985.

Mao Tse-tung. *Quotations from Chairman Mao Tse-tung*. New York: Bantam Books, 1967.

———. *Selected Works*. 5 vols. New York: International Publishers, 1954–56.

Marx, Karl. *Critique of the Gotha Program*. New York: International Publishers, 1938.

———. *Early Writings*. New York: Vintage Books, 1975.

———. *The Eighteenth Brumaire of Louis Bonaparte*. New York: International Publishers, n.d.

———. *Pre-Capitalist Economic Formations*. New York: International Publishers, 1965.

———. *Surveys from Exile*. New York: Vintage Books, 1974.

Marx, Karl, and Friedrich Engels. *The German Ideology. Parts I and III*. New York: International Publishers, 1947.

———. *On Colonialism*. New York: International Publishers, 1972.

———. *Werke*. 43 vols. Berlin: Dietz Verlag, 1956–68.

Meyer, Alfred G. *Leninism*. New York: Praeger, 1962.

New York Times. December 28, 1989; April 13, 1990; August 10, 1990; May 29, 1991; December 9, 1991; April 7, 1992.

Nolan, Mary. *Social Democracy and Society. Working-Class Radicalism in Düsseldorf, 1890–1920*. Cambridge: Cambridge University Press, 1981.

Oldenburg-Januschau, Elard von. *Erinnerungen*. Leipzig: Koehler & Amelang, 1936.

Parvus [Alexander Helphand]. "Die gegenwärtige politische Lage Russlands und die Aussichten für die Zukunft." *Die Neue Zeit* 24/2 (1906): 108–20.

Pawlowitsch, Michael. "Die grosse chinesische Revolution." *Die Neue Zeit* 30/1 (1911–12): 372–85, 494–506, 557–70.

———. "Die revolutionäre Bewegung und die politischen Parteien im heutigen China." *Die Neue Zeit* 29/2 (1911): 37–42, 80–84.

Perlez, Jane. "A New Chance for a Fractured Land." *New York Times Magazine*, September 22, 1991: 49–51, 56–57, 74–76, 85.

Plamenatz, John. *German Marxism and Russian Communism*. New York: Harper & Row, 1965.

"Platform of the Viet-Nam Lao Dong Party." *People's China* 3, no. 9 (May 1, 1951): supp.

Ra'anan, Uri. "Moscow and the 'Third World.' " *Problems of Communism* 14, no. 1 (January–February 1965): 22–31.

Ratliff, William E. *Castroism and Communism in Latin America, 1959–1976*. Washington, D.C.: American Enterprise Institute, 1976.

Ritter, Gerhard A. *Wahlgeschichtliches Arbeitsbuch*. Munich: Beck, 1980.

Roca, Blas. "The Cuban Revolution in Action." *World Marxist Review* 2, no. 8 (August 1959): 16–22.

Roth, Guenther. *The Social Democrats in Imperial Germany*. Totowa, N.J.: Bedminster Press, 1963.

Schorske, Carl F. *German Social Democracy, 1905–1917*. Cambridge, Mass.: Harvard University Press, 1955.

Schram, Stuart R. "On the Quotations." In Mao Tse-tung, *Quotations from Chairman Mao Tse-tung*.

———. *The Political Thought of Mao Tse-tung*. New York: Praeger, 1963.

Schwartz, Benjamin I. *Chinese Communism and the Rise of Mao*. Cambridge, Mass.: Harvard University Press, 1951.

Schwarz, Max, ed. *M.d.R. Biographisches Handbuch der Reichstage*. Hannover: Verlag für Literatur und Zeitgeschichte, 1965.

Seliger, Martin. *Ideology and Politics*. London: Allen and Unwin, 1976.

———. *The Marxist Conception of Ideology*. Cambridge: Cambridge University Press, 1977.

Skocpol, Theda. *States and Social Revolutions*. New York: Cambridge University Press, 1979.

Steenson, Gary P. *After Marx, Before Lenin. Marxism and Socialist Working Class Parties in Europe, 1884–1914*. Pittsburgh: University of Pittsburgh Press, 1991.

Suval, Stanley. *Electoral Politics in Wilhemine Germany*. Chapel Hill: University of North Carolina Press, 1985.

This Week in Germany. New York: German Information Center, December 20, 1991.

Trotsky, Leon. *The Permanent Revolution*. New York: Pioneer Publishers, 1931.

———. *The Permanent Revolution* and *Results and Prospects*, New York: Merit Publishers, 1969.

Tucker, Robert C., ed. *The Marx-Engels Reader*. 2d ed. New York: W. W. Norton, 1978.

van der Sprenkel, Otto B., ed. *New China: Three Views*. New York: John Day, 1951.

Vogel, Bernhard, Dieter Nohlen, and Rainer-Olaf Schultze. *Wahlen in Deutschland*. Berlin: de Gruyter, 1971.

Zeitlin, Maurice, and Richard Earl Ratcliff. "Research Methods for the Analysis of the Internal Structure of Dominant Classes: The Case of Landlords and Capitalists in Chile." *Latin American Research Review* 10, no. 3 (Fall 1975): 5–61.

Zierold, Paul. "Die Revolution in Mexiko." *Die Neue Zeit* 29/2 (1911): 396–402.

Index

About the Author

JOHN H. KAUTSKY is Professor Emeritus of Political Science at Washington University in St. Louis. He is the author of several books, including most recently *Karl Kautsky: Marxism, Revolution, and Democracy* (1993).